BENCH RULES

A Guide to Success
On and Off the Bench

Kevin Christensen

To the loves of my life: my beautiful wife Megan and our greatest joy, our daughter Hannah.

To Dad, Mom, Brad, Grandma and Grandpa for the love, support and inspiration you have always given me.

To the three most influential basketball coaches in my life: Justin Clymo, Pat Fuscaldo and Rich Shayewitz. I would have been lost without your guidance.

Table of Contents

Foreword

By Vince Inglima

It was early in the second half of our game against Cal State Monterey Bay, and things were not looking good. We were trailing by double digits to a team that had never beaten us in the history of the school. No one was playing well. Coach Fuscaldo was frantically searching for something to ignite our team. After all, if we lost that game, we could kiss any chance of making the national tournament goodbye.

With about 15 minutes remaining in the game, Coach made what some would view as a desperate move. He grabbed the last guy off our bench and put him in the game. To an onlooker, it might have appeared like he was giving up. After all, on most college teams, that chubby kid at the end of the bench is just there to wave a towel and get good grades. But that was not the case on this team. In his first 30 seconds on the floor, he had already stolen a pass and hit a deep three pointer. He continued on to score 17 points down the stretch to rally us to a great come-from-behind win.

I had transferred to Sonoma State at the start of my junior year of college, and this was my first encounter with the magic of Kevin Christensen. There would be so many more games like that one the following season that it almost became the norm. In my two years, Kevin went from rarely stepping foot on the court to a starter on a championship team. And if you didn't watch the games, you wouldn't have noticed a single change in him.

In *BENCH RULES*, Kevin talks about controlling your effort and attitude on and off the court, and he epitomized that during his playing career. He was our 14th man for a long time, but his good nature and fierce competitiveness established a culture of unity on our team. He thrived in seemingly the worst role anyone could have on a team, and we were all the better for it. How could anyone else complain about a role, if he was willing to accept his?

As the years pass, and I look back on those days of playing college basketball, I relish the feeling I got from being on that team. A group of guys who, despite their differences in one way or another, were singularly focused on a common goal. A group of kids who understood the importance of sacrificing part of yourself for the betterment of the group. That attitude was born and nurtured on our team by the eternally positive energy brought by one player, every day, without fail.

BENCH RULES is not just a book about basketball. Its lessons can be utilized in any team environment. It is about creating a culture of positivity that leads to individual and group success. It's often thought that a team's culture comes from the top down, established by the coaches on a team, or the managers in an office. But *BENCH RULES* shows us how the supposedly lowest member of a group can have the biggest impact. And in doing so, create a path for himself to achieve his dreams.

With my playing days behind me, I continue to fuel my passion for the game as a coach at Cal State Monterey Bay (and yes, we have since beaten Sonoma State!). At the beginning of every season, I ask each of my players, "How will you react if you are our 14th player?" I get a variety of answers, some good and some bad. But I have yet to encounter another Kevin Christensen. He demonstrates passion, resolve, and how to get the most out of every situation. Hopefully, *BENCH RULES* will teach more players how to achieve greatness through positivity.

Vince Inglima, 2011

-Assistant Men's Basketball Coach, Cal State Monterey Bay

-Professional Basketball Player, Dandenong Rangers (Australia)

-All-American Basketball Player, Sonoma State University

A Note from the Author:

I initially wrote this book with the intention of helping the non-starters on a basketball team find ways in which they could help their team. I specifically targeted those who may only play a few minutes a game if at all.

As the book took its form I realized that it would help any player on a basketball team. In fact, the focus group who read the early drafts of the book insist that the lessons within can, and should, be applied outside of basketball as well.

While this book is told from a basketball perspective, I believe that anyone can take lessons from it and apply them to their own endeavors. I did not relate my message to other sports or business because that is not my experience, and would not have been authentic.

I hope you also feel that while my story is told from a basketball perspective, the lessons and experiences can transcend basketball, sports in general, and can help any individual, team, or organization navigate adversity as it arises.

Kevin Christensen

A Guide to Success

Every player dreams of becoming a superstar on the basketball court. Millions of players at all levels, from youth to professional, are constantly striving to be the best player on their team, in their league and even in the world. With so many wanting to be the next Kobe Bryant or LeBron James, what happens when their dream is turned into a reality of sitting on the bench? For most players this is a time filled with mixed feelings and emotions as they try to find their way in a situation for which they are unprepared. Suddenly, they are being asked to perform in a role that is unlike any they had thought they would find themselves a part of.

No one who aspires to be the best in their sport hopes they become a bench player. No one puts in the time and effort to work on their game so they can sit on the bench and watch others play. This often leaves bench players frustrated and wondering what they have to do to be successful. They are trying to figure out what the necessary qualities are to perform on a team in this role. Most importantly, every bench player wants to know what they have to do to get on the court on game day.

On most teams in the sport of basketball, there are more players who begin the game on the bench than the five who actually start on the court. Yet there is little guidance that is given to bench players; often they are pushed to the background while the "best" players on each team are given the most attention, highest value and most of the praise. This is why it is essential for players to learn how much of an impact they can have on the success of a team, even if they are not the "superstar" they always wanted to be. Every coach and player knows that no team is ever truly their best unless everyone is developing and reaching their full potential. This potential should not only be judged by how a player performs on the court, but also if they become their best as a teammate and person along the way. It is no secret that the growth of everyone on a team, on and off the court, is critical to the success of any team.

That's why *BENCH RULES* is here. It is a guide for every player who desires to thrive in their reserve role; it is a way to find success in a situation with which many struggle. I know because I was in this role. I was the last player on the bench for my college basketball team until late in my junior season. When you add my redshirt year to that equation, that is almost four of my five years as a college basketball player spent on the bench. It was a time I struggled to find my identity as a player and team member. I was on a roller coaster ride of ups and downs, as I had never experienced anything like being on the bench. But it was these moments that helped teach me how to contribute to our team's success in many different ways. It was this time that helped prepare and shape me for a future of success on the court. My time on the bench was a teacher of many different lessons and I made myself better for having these experiences instead of letting them bring me down.

Here in these pages lies a way for every player and team to become their best, to find different ways to become better and stronger. *BENCH RULES* is an acronym with each letter representing a different topic that focuses on how to be more of a contributor on a basketball team and the good news is that it does not only apply to bench players. I used these rules to guide me when I became a starter in my senior year in college as well. In fact, any player who wants to be their best on the court can apply its lessons to their own situation, from superstar to last man on the bench. Every rule is coupled with stories and observations from my college basketball playing career. They will offer examples on what I had to do to become my best so I could become a better player, person and a contributing member of my basketball team in every role that I played.

The Victory Cigar

With less than a minute left in the second half, we had pushed our halftime lead from ten to seventeen. Like every other game that season, I had been watching the rest of my teammates play from the seat at the end of the bench. Everyone who had stepped on the court that night for my college basketball team, the Sonoma State Seawolves, had played hard to extend the halftime advantage. Now with very little time remaining, the outcome of the game was clearly decided. It now reached the moment where it was safe to clear the bench; it was a chance for both coaches to put in little used reserves and let the game play out in "garbage time."

As a freshman that season, these were the occasions I actually got on the court; it was the only time when I heard my name called to check in the game. My entrance on the court was so rare that it became symbolic. It signaled victory for our team and was a feel good moment for everyone in the gym. It was the equivalent to former coaching great Red Auerbach lighting a cigar on the sideline when it was apparent that his legendary Celtics teams of the 60's had their games won. I became that image for our team; I was our "victory cigar." I had now reached a new low as a player. As a young player, I always thought I would be the best player on every team I was ever on. I never dreamed that I would be coming off the bench. But reality was even worse than that, because now I was the last player off the bench!

Becoming that last player off the bench was new to me. Prior to my arrival at Sonoma State I had been a starter and top two leading scorer every year in high school. In my senior year I played almost every minute of every game and finished the year with an average of just over 17 points. But now I was in my second year at Sonoma State University, my official freshman season after I spent the previous year as a redshirt, and I couldn't get off the bench. I was feeling lost because the only time that I got in the game was when it didn't matter. I never had a chance to make a difference in meaningful game situations. There were a few instances when I would show I could be more than the last player off the bench, but those moments were few and far in between. They were just glimpses of what, perhaps, I might be able to become if I could find a way to earn more minutes, if I could somehow figure out what it took to get on the court when it mattered.

I knew that I could be more of a contributor, and I definitely knew I wanted to play more, but I was unsure how to go about it. Everything I had done up to that point seemed to have little effect on the minutes I was receiving during games. I would constantly ask myself, *How can my role change, how can I become a contributor on the court?* As I would find out over the next few years, it would take a combination of many different variables for me to become more than the "victory cigar." What I had to do was adapt and follow the *BENCH RULES*.

When I put the ten *BENCH RULES* into action, I transformed myself from being the last player off the bench to the starting point guard and all-conference selection on a championship team when I was a senior. I would then cap off my career as a basketball player by signing a contract to play professionally in Europe. I had completely turned my fortunes around because of the actions I took to improve my skills and change my point of view when I was struggling on the bench. I stopped looking at my situation as a bench player negatively and found joy and self worth in my new role because of the many changes I had made by using the *BENCH RULES*.

While I was on my journey and striving to find a way to become more of a contributor on the court, I also found that the *BENCH RULES* made me a better teammate and person. When I put just one of the rules into action, I instantly earned more respect and credibility from my coaches and teammates, and I made contributions in areas I didn't even realize were important. That's why *BENCH RULES* is not singularly focused on increasing your minutes on the court (that will happen if you follow them), but you will also find you will have an impact on your team in ways other than with traditional statistics.

Because of the *BENCH RULES*, I made contributions to my team in so many different ways that I was voted the "Most Inspirational Player" every year I played at Sonoma State. Even the years I rarely got to play in games, I still had an impact, and everyone around me took notice. Because of that, I left a significant mark on the program that will always be remembered. After my final season, the program renamed the award the "Kevin Christensen Most Inspirational Player

Award." I didn't "wow" everybody in the gym with my athleticism and skills, but I made them recognize that I was going to be a major contributor to our basketball team whether I was a starter or if I didn't play at all. Any player at any level who uses the strategies in this book, and learns from its situations, can have the same impact that I had while I was a college player. By following the rules, you will be putting a plan into action that will make you better in every aspect of the game and you and your team will improve in more ways than you ever thought possible.

If you were to ask anyone who knows me, they would probably tell you that I drastically overachieved as a player, that I got the most I could out of my abilities and then some. This happened because I was forced to find different ways to get better or I would have had to continue in my suffering on the bench, settling for minutes that were insignificant to the outcome of the game. My journey took more time and work than I ever thought it would, but the lessons I learned from it can help anyone improve and find value on their team, whether they are the most talented player or sit the bench like I did.

Believe in Yourself

The most important trait you must possess as an athlete is self-confidence. When you believe in yourself, you will have confidence that cannot be shaken no matter what kind of challenges you face. You can only begin to achieve your goals on the court if you first believe that you have the capacity to achieve them. This belief is the basis for any great accomplishment in sports.

Competitive athletics is filled with constant mental and physical challenges from opponents, teammates, coaches and even yourself. It is up to you to deal with the ups and downs you will face by being a believer in how great you are and how much greater you can become. There are moments where every player has to deal with adversity and their success is always determined by how they respond to it. You can decide to believe in yourself and successfully handle the daily challenges, or you can doubt yourself and let the challenges get the best of you.

Believing in yourself is especially important for bench players. Those who come off the bench and do not receive consistent minutes face different challenges than the players who see the majority of time on the court during a game. As a bench player, there are different scenarios that will force you to look inside yourself for the necessary strength to continue to have confidence in your abilities and perform successfully on the court.

There are times when you have great practice sessions, situations where you feel like you outplayed the players in front of you and your confidence will be sky high. Then game day rolls around and you only play a few minutes, or you might not play at all. There will also be practices where it seems like you cannot do anything right and your coach is always critical of your play. Another day you will get in the game and be playing well, making a solid contribution to your team, then after only a few minutes, sometimes it could be seconds, you are subbed out and you are back on the bench.

This is the reality of a player in a reserve role. While you think you can have a huge impact on the game, there may be a match-up your coach doesn't like or they may decide that another player can give them more on the court at that time. No matter what your coach's logic is, and you may have no clue what it is, all of these moments can be extremely frustrating. They can turn into situations that make it easy to lose your confidence and can lead to you starting to doubt yourself.

As a bench player, all kinds of different thoughts can creep into your head if you let them. You are constantly searching for the reasoning behind why you are not playing. You may even try to be logical with yourself about your abilities, thinking that you just aren't good enough. This seems obvious because if you were better, then you would play more regularly. Or you might be on the other end of the spectrum, blaming your coach, insisting that he has no idea what he is doing because in your mind, he must be crazy not to play you. But no matter what your situation is, you cannot get caught up in any negative thoughts. You have to look at the things you are doing right and not let any factors outside of your control influence how you feel about yourself. This is so important because if you do not believe in yourself, no one else will. A player without confidence in themselves is one who is on a path to self-destruction. If you let any doubt enter your mind, then it will translate to your play on the court and neither you nor your team will benefit.

Always Think Positively

In my first three and a half years as a college basketball player, I got very little playing time. There were plenty of moments where my skills were challenged and I started doubting myself, but this was especially true during my first year at Sonoma State, which was my redshirt season. As a redshirt I got to practice with the team every day, but I was not eligible to play in games. That season I was just out of high school, I was 18 years old playing against guys who were anywhere from one to seven years older. All of the players I faced in practice had more experience playing at a higher level of competition; they were all bigger, faster and stronger. This translated to major problems for me on the court, but the most glaring as an aspiring point guard was with turning the ball over.

The speed of play was so much faster than it was in high school and that, combined with my lack of strength, made it hard to take care of the basketball. I was playing so terribly that I was not allowed to participate in some of the drills in practice. The coaches actually told me to get out of the line and just watch. I obviously started doubting myself because if I couldn't practice, how could I ever expect to be used in a game? It was an absolute embarrassment for me. I knew I had to find a way to turn my play around and it started with my confidence and belief in myself.

I quickly realized that by doubting my abilities I had put negative thoughts in my head and it showed in my play on the court. I didn't believe I could make any positive things happen and because of that I continued to make bad plays. Every day I went to the gym, my thoughts turned more and more negative, and suddenly the doubt in myself was snowballing. Every time I made a mistake I felt like I wanted to dig a hole in the gym and hide in it; my fear of failure was encompassing my every thought. But once I started to focus on the positive things I was doing in practice (believe me, I had to look hard for them), I stopped being so hard on myself and my outlook changed. Just that simple adjustment in my thinking led to better play in practice and translated to gaining more confidence in myself with every passing day.

Part of this transformation in thinking was that I remembered I was at Sonoma State because I had been a good player before I got there. I had to remember that I had been successful on the court many times before. It was hard to continue to think positively, especially when I felt I was doing more bad than good in practice. However, I let the good moments encourage me and used the moments I failed as learning experiences and motivation to improve. After a few weeks, I had found different ways to protect the ball and not cause as many turnovers and it was enough to be more

11

competitive in practice. It also led to more chances on the court, as the coaching staff no longer had to take me out of drills. I was now able to compete in all aspects of practice without slowing everyone else down. Although I still had a very long way to go to be good enough to consistently make positive plays happen on the court, I was showing improvement, and suddenly my game and confidence were heading in a positive direction.

Never Lose Confidence in Your Abilities

Two years later, when I was a sophomore athletically, I had a moment that was more challenging for me as a player than any other I had ever experienced. My head coach challenged me in a way that could have broken me as a player and ended my basketball career at Sonoma State. I was forced to believe in myself or the challenges from my coach could have gotten the best of me.

After many games of limited playing time and sitting on the bench, I finally got a real chance to play substantial minutes against a division three opponent. It was early in the season and our roster was full of younger players. The two point guards in front of me in the rotation were not playing well, so I got a chance to show what I could do in a game situation. I would end up playing solid for our team that night, but more importantly, I played well enough where I was in at the end, playing the minutes that mattered the most to the outcome of the game. Unfortunately, we would eventually go on to lose in overtime, but I still felt good about my performance on the court. I had hit a few shots and made good decisions as the team's point guard and I left the gym that night thinking I was a bright spot in an otherwise disappointing overtime loss.

The next day in practice we did very little with the basketball. Our coach was so furious from the loss the night before that the practice session was filled with nothing but running sprints and defensive drills without a ball. Our coach also took time in between each sprint and drill to let us all know how he felt about our progress as a team and individuals. At one point our whole team was lined up on the baseline as our head coach had each team member, one by one, step out while he gave us his thoughts on our development as basketball players. As I finally stepped out to hear what our coach had to say, I was extremely nervous because he had been absolutely brutal with the players before me. He was venting his frustration from our loss the night before and as all the players knew, our coach was not going to hold anything back. I was, however, also feeling some confidence because I thought I had played well in our previous game. I thought that if he had anything to say to me, maybe he would be complimentary of my time on the court.

Once our coach began to speak, I suddenly realized that nothing I had done had changed his opinion of me. I had a few meetings with him in the previous two years where he told me how I could improve, but now he was more frustrated, which led to him being even more direct. I will never forget the words he said: "Kevin, you have all the heart in the world. You practice harder than any player on this team, but your lack of athleticism and speed puts you at a huge disadvantage on defense. I don't think you can guard my mother and she is 70 years old. You may never be able to play for me."

No matter how much confidence I had at the time, this was very hard for me to hear, especially the end of his short rant when he said, "You may never be able to play for me." Those words echoed in my head. I thought I had showed great progress the night before, but more importantly, since I had started in the program two years prior I knew I had become a much better player. All the time and work I had put in seemed to be lost on my coach, but I couldn't let it bring me down. I had a strong belief in myself that had developed since my first year at Sonoma State. I had the inner strength to take my coach's words simply as a challenge to get better and not as a self-fulfilling prophecy for my future in the game of basketball.

This moment could have affected me negatively, as it did some of my teammates, but I kept my confidence. I knew I could push through this obstacle and continue to progress as a player. I wasn't going to be sensitive and let my feelings get hurt, I was going to turn this situation into something positive for my team and myself. When I finished my playing career at Sonoma State, this was one of the moments I looked back fondly upon because it was the moment that symbolized I had developed a strong belief in myself. I didn't let my coach's words and opinions affect how I felt as a player or person. I didn't let them break me, but instead I used them as motivation to prove to him I could do more than he thought I could.

This was a moment that also turned out to be one of the turning points for our team over the course of my time at

Sonoma State. The core group of us who were in the gym that day persevered and won our conference for the first time ever just one and a half years later. It was probably my coach's plan to have this speech motivate us and challenge us to be better, but if I had not believed in my abilities, his opinion given to me that day may have turned out to be true; I may have never been able to play for him. Instead, I let it motivate me to become a champion on the court.

Conclusion

These were just two of the times as a player where my confidence was challenged. As a bench player, or any player for that matter, you are challenged every day. That is what being on a competitive team in a competitive sport is all about. I had games where I would hit five three pointers and the next night I played one minute. There were practices where I was outplaying the guy in front of me and I didn't play at all in the next game. Our coach would come up to me after some games and tell me, "I was going to play you last night, but the right match-up never happened." I didn't let any of it have an effect on my confidence because I believed in my abilities and knew what I was capable of on the court. I just kept working on becoming even better. Without that belief and confidence it would have been easy to give up. Instead, I expected great things from myself and because of that I never let myself settle for being anything but great.

Tips for Success

- Always believe in yourself and your abilities. A player without confidence is one who is easily discouraged and becomes non-productive when things aren't going their way.

- The power of positive thinking will drive you to improving yourself. Negative thoughts and emotions will translate to your play on the court.

- Focus on what you are doing well. No matter how small an accomplishment may be, let it fuel you to continue improving.

- If you do not expect great things from yourself then you will settle for being mediocre.

Extra Work

If you want to become a better player, and have a bigger role for your team on the court, then there is no better way to do this than to improve your skills. To improve, you have to put in the work. This chapter is not simply called "Extra Practice" because, while that is important, you will need to do more. You will need to put in more work, not only in the gym, but also the weight room, the film room and the classroom. You have to challenge yourself to be a better player because if you are not working at it, someone else is, and when you two meet, they will be better than you. This thought should be the main motivation for any player to work on improving their game on the court.

The year can be divided into two parts, and each requires a unique approach to improve as a player. The things you can do to improve will be different during the season than when you are in the off-season, but both will play huge factors in your quest to become the player you always dreamed you could be.

In-season

The biggest aspect of improving during the season is finding extra time outside of your team's practice to work on your game. Your goal, especially if you don't get a lot of minutes, should be to work on your individual skills more than anyone else. You don't really have any choice; there is a reason you are not playing the minutes you desire, so you have to improve. It is a process that must be maximized on a daily basis. You should ask yourself at the end of each day, "What have I done today to get better and separate myself from other players on my team, in my league or even in the world?" If you can do this, and hold yourself accountable, then you can end your day knowing you gave your all to reach your goals on the court.

In the midst of a season, a majority of your coach's practice plan has to be dedicated to team development and strategies. Therefore, it will not leave as much time for you to work on your individual skill development. If you are not a big contributor, it may also mean you get fewer repetitions in practice than other players and in this case you have to find your own time to make up for it. How much you improve truly comes down to the extra time and effort you are willing to sacrifice outside of your team's practices.

Before you start to put in the extra work, you need to make sure that the extra time you spend improving is focusing on utilizing the skills and aspects of your game that need the most attention. For this, it is imperative that you do not leave it up to your own judgment on what skills need the most help. You should seek the advice of your coaches and teammates to see what areas they think you can improve upon. These two groups of people see you in the gym every day and have a vested interest in you becoming a better player. Because of this, you should expect honesty and some things you may not want or expect to hear.

It is very important that you have an open mind and are able to accept what they tell you about how you can improve. This can be intimidating because you are asking someone to tell you what you do not do well on the court. Many people will hesitate to ask this kind of question because there is a feeling of vulnerability when you open yourself up to criticism. But if you can find the courage to ask, listen to what they say, accept it and work on it, then you will be better. The first group of people you should ask is the members of your coaching staff. They are so important because they are in control of the team, they decide what the rotation will be, and the wins and losses will go on their record. Therefore, no one will have a better idea of what they want to see you do on the court than your coaches. You may even be surprised with what they have to say. After your coaching staff, your teammates are an excellent source because they are the ones with whom you actually play against every day. They have a perspective unlike any other because they know your strengths, weaknesses and tendencies on the court. Both your coaches and teammates should be able to give you excellent insight into how you can maximize your time in the gym.

Work Harder and Smarter Outside of Your Practices

As a redshirt freshman, there were many things that I needed to improve. As I mentioned earlier, the most glaring for me, especially since I was a point guard, was that for the first two months of practice I kept turning the ball over. The older players on the team made me look so bad during practice that I couldn't even participate in most scrimmages because of my inability to handle the basketball. So when I went to ask one of the assistant coaches what I needed to work on, I was surprised when he told me, "On the ball defense." After he saw the puzzled look on my face, he went on to explain further and told me that it was obvious I had trouble handling ball pressure, but if I couldn't get quicker with my feet and keep offensive players in front of me, then it would be difficult for our coach to ever play me (which I found out the hard way just a year later when he told me I couldn't guard his 70-year-old mother).

After this conversation with our assistant, not only was it clear what I needed to work on individually, but I also found out what aspect of the game our coaching staff put a lot of importance towards. I was a new player to the program and this information was very valuable. Because of this simple five minute conversation, I knew what needed to be done for me to reach my goals of one day being on the court. It would take me a few years before I became ready to contribute in these situations without being a defensive liability, but I was aware of where I had to improve so I could start to earn more minutes.

Over the course of my five years at Sonoma State, I had several instances where my defensive abilities were questioned and it was a constant battle to get better on the defensive end. This would involve a lot of my extra work being dedicated to becoming quicker, stronger and smarter. I worked on my foot speed in the gym, my strength in the weight room and watched game film to try and improve my mind and get a better grasp on our defensive schemes. All three factors led to my improvement on defense and eventually made me ready to play consistently in my last two seasons. I never became an outstanding on-ball defender because I was never as athletic or quick as other players, but I made up for that deficiency by finding ways to be more efficient, savvier, and craftier on the defensive end of the floor.

The kind of skills that a player needs to improve can be much shorter fixes than what took me years to develop. For example, I also worked on my ball handling after practice every day for 20 minutes and within a few weeks I was able to handle the pressure from my teammates when I was in practice. Because of my willingness to put in extra time outside of our practice, I earned more repetitions and opportunities in practice, and my confidence and skills began to grow. As a redshirt who didn't play in games, this was extremely important for me and the lesson continued well into my senior year.

The time outside of practice that you use to improve may also be spent sharpening an aspect of the game that you already do well. My final season I would make 150 shots after practice every day, and this contributed greatly to my shooting percentage in games. I was already a solid shooter from the outside, but the extra time helped make me even better. That season we were in a run for our first ever conference championship and a lot of our success was due to the commitment we gave in practice to our team's defensive schemes and strategies. Our advantage over other teams was our knowledge of what they tried to do on offense and how we were going to stop it. That meant preparation for our next opponent involved a lot of defensive work. We did have some time in practice to work on individual skills like dribbling, passing, shooting and footwork, but I knew I needed more of it to perform at my highest level.

Everyone on the team took that same viewpoint that year and we were all better for it, individually and collectively, because we were willing to put in extra work outside of our practices. I believe it was that extra time that contributed to the outstanding results for our team; it was the difference between second place and winning the conference championship banner that hangs in our gym today. One or two points, or one possession often decides games, one player can be the difference and this difference can be putting in the extra work that others do not.

Off-season

The off-season is the best time of year to become a better individual player. There is nothing else to worry about during this time of the year other than improving your own game. If you are a high school level player or below, then you may spend time playing in summer leagues with your team, but the overall focus should still be your individual development as a basketball player.

As discussed previously, it is so important to get advice from your coaches and teammates on what areas of your game you should improve. After these two groups, you may seek the advice of those outside of your team because sometimes they may see things from a different perspective that may be credible, but remember, your coaches and teammates are the opinions in which you should put the most value. A conversation I had with some of my teammates and coaches made me realize that I had to improve in the off-season, not just with my basketball skills, but also with my conditioning.

Improve Your Conditioning and Skills

As I explained earlier, it took me years to finally become good enough defensively to earn just a few minutes of playing time. I had to become quicker on the court and one of the reasons I was so slow is that I was slightly overweight. The harsh reality that I had to face and the criticism I opened myself up to involved the condition my body was in. I was simply carrying around too many extra pounds. It got so bad that one of my coaches even gave me the nickname "The Snowman" because of my round shape (and pasty white skin).

I had faced small weight issues my whole life, so when I was forced to realize that I needed to lose weight, it stung, just as it always had. It can be very hard to face the truth, but you have to if you want to get better. As I said before, the criticism you receive you must listen to and accept, then you must work on getting around, over or through whatever obstacle it is that is in front of you. After I finally came to accept that I needed to drop some weight, I decided I needed a lifestyle change. I had to avoid the drive through window and change my diet. I also committed myself to working harder in the gym during the summer. I woke up at 5:30AM to lift weights and get 100-200 shots in before going to work for eight hours. I would then end my day with a three mile run in the Sacramento heat, followed by more work in the gym on my basketball skills. I also started writing a daily food journal and kept myself honest with what I put in my body.

After just three months of this schedule, I dropped 10 pounds while adding muscular weight and I became a better basketball player because my body was in better condition. When I got back to campus, everything in our fall conditioning program became easier and practices were not as physically challenging to me. While other guys were exhausted in practice, I was able to stay focused and work on my skills more effectively. Because of these changes, I was a different player and began to do things on the court I had never done before. I was defending players I previously wasn't able to guard and began beating people to loose balls and on sprints down the court. After my sophomore year, when I finally made these changes to both my eating habits and workout plan, I found that because of my commitment to it for just three months, it helped turn my basketball career around.

I always cherished each off-season because of the opportunities it presented to get better. I loved the off-season season so much that it was the time of year I found to be the most fun. The season is truly a grind, but when it got to the off-season, I enjoyed it because it was a chance to separate myself from other players through hard work. It was my goal to outwork every other player during the summer. I really had no choice, I felt like I had to if I was going to get more playing time. I also remembered that every day I got better, my team got better. I was obsessed with becoming my best every day because I knew that if I was not improving, somebody else was. I knew that extra hour I put in at the gym and those extra 150 shots at the end of my workout could be the difference between first and second place, or playing in games and sitting the bench. I turned out to be right on both counts, as it ended up being the difference between being an on-the-court contributing member of a championship team and what I had been in the previous years; the player at the end of the bench.

Conclusion

There is no doubt that you have to constantly strive to improve as a player, especially if you are on the bench. You cannot settle for only working on your game when everyone else does or on the days that you feel good. You have to do more than anyone else. By making it a priority and developing a habit of doing it all the time, you will be on your way to becoming the best player you can possibly be. So make a plan to put in the extra work others are not willing to in the off-season and during the season. Then stick with that plan and watch your game and status on your team rise to another level.

Tips for Success

- To become a better player you have to put in extra work in the off-season and during the season.

- Extra work means improving in the gym, the weight room, and in your mental capacity for the game.

- In-season you have to find time outside of your team's regularly scheduled practice to work on the necessary skills you need to become a better player.

- The off-season should be dedicated to becoming bigger, faster, stronger and smarter in all aspects of the game.

- Your coaches will have the best ideas for what areas can use the most improvement for you as an individual player. Your teammates rank a high second on this list.

- Your success on the court will be a direct result of the extra work you put into becoming a better player.

Never Quit

When you put in the time and effort it takes to be on a team, it can be difficult if you are not achieving the results you desire. Every competitive person wants to be the best. When you are successful, everything feels right. You feel like the work you put in and the sacrifices you make are all worthwhile. At some point, though, you are going to be in a situation where you do not get what you want out of your commitment to the game of basketball. It could happen as a youth player, in high school, maybe in college and for some it may not happen until they are professionals. This is when the true test of an individual occurs. It is easy to be a positive player, teammate and person when things are going your way. But what happens when you are challenged? What happens when success on the court does not come so easily?

For many players, when things do not go their way they start to think about giving up; this is the moment they contemplate quitting because it is the easiest and quickest solution to their problems. Quitting on your team can come in different forms, it can mean you physically remove yourself from your team or it can be quitting mentally. No matter which form of quitting occurs, you have to realize the negative effect your decision will have on you personally and on everyone involved with your team. Your decision to quit will speak volumes about who you are as a person and will change your teams future, and maybe even the course of your life.

Realize the Value of Being Part of a Team

Between my freshman and sophomore years, I was at a crossroads in my college basketball career. I had been in the Sonoma State program for two years and had only played sparingly. I had been recruited over every year, and this summer the coaches were looking to find yet another point guard, definite signs that my progress did not impress them. There were so many legitimate reasons, in my head anyway, that told me I should quit playing basketball. I had also been dealing with a nagging six-year old injury with my shooting arm that had become worse. But most importantly, I felt like I was not getting much out of the sacrifice I was making to be a part of my team. I was going to practice every day with a great attitude and work ethic, but I wasn't getting the benefit of the time on the court I thought I deserved. I felt like I could do what any other player on the court was doing and my year-round commitment to basketball was looking like it was a huge waste of my time and energy.

I went back and forth on the issue of quitting for several weeks that summer, but it wasn't until I talked to my high school coach that I finally realized the correct course of action. My high school coach was a mentor and role model of mine and when he spoke, I always listened. He quickly got me to realize how lucky I was to be a college basketball player. He reminded me how fortunate I was to get a chance to go to practice every day and play a game I loved. There are so few people who get the opportunity to do something they are passionate about, so few get to live their dream and I was doing it on a daily basis. This thought can be lost on a lot of players when they are feeling down about their situation. It can be so easy to focus on the negative aspects that you end up forgetting what the bigger picture looks like. You can get so caught up with the everyday business of being frustrated with basketball that you suddenly stop realizing how lucky you really are to be able to be a part of a team in a sport that you love.

A lot of people wish they had the ability and talent to be a part of a sports team at any level, but especially in college. The same was true for me. I had worked tirelessly in the gym for years so I could become good enough to realize my dream of playing college basketball and now to quit I would be giving up on that dream. My high school coach knew I had an incredible passion for the game and without basketball in my life, I would not be the same person. He knew I would have had a huge void in my life that could not have been filled by anything except basketball.

With the quick change of perspective, I forever lost my thoughts of quitting, and to this day I feel ashamed that I ever had them. I can't even imagine not having the memories and experiences that came with my last three years as a college basketball player. They ended up being the ultimate reward of so many years of commitment to the game and without them my life wouldn't be the same.

Now that I am done playing, I would give almost anything to go back to my days as a player. It was those times, when I got to compete on the basketball court every day, that I will never forget. Even the days I struggled the most, when I felt down about myself as a player, those are the moments I wish I could relive. It was then I learned how resilient and strong I was as a person and I found I had the will power to overcome any obstacle. If I had quit I would never have experienced how to get past the challenges I face and I would have never realized how these moments were the ones that taught me the most about what it takes to become a better player, teammate and person.

Quitting Affects Everyone

If you still feel like there is no hope for you, like no matter what you do you are going to be miserable by remaining on your team, please think about your teammates. If you quit, you are quitting on them, and your decision affects their future as well. Whether you are a starter or the last player off the bench, there is a chemistry that develops on a team as the season progresses, there is a dependency on one another that can be easily disrupted.

During my freshman year at Sonoma State, two weeks before the end of the regular season, our starting shooting guard quit because he did not agree with how the coaching staff was handling our team. At this point of our season we had four games left and we were making our final stretch run at qualifying for the NCAA tournament. When he quit, our whole rotation changed and everyone on the team was forced to adjust and try to make up for it. This was the last chance for the seniors on our team to play college basketball; it was the climax of their four years of hard work and dedication to the game and it was forever altered by one person's decision to leave the team.

The timing of his quitting couldn't have been worse. Though we ended up still qualifying for the NCAA tournament, we were not the same team we had been just a few weeks prior. We got a lower seed than we would have had if we had finished our season stronger and we lost our opening round game in embarrassing fashion. While it was not all our ex-teammate's fault, it certainly did not help that we did not have one of our most veteran and talented players for our late season run. Instead of having him as our starter, suddenly his back-up was thrown into the lineup and our bench was now weaker, too. His single act of quitting had a domino effect that threw off our team balance. All of it ended up changing the course of our season and we underachieved as a team because of it.

Quitting can also bring trouble for a team even when little used bench players decide to take this route. Some players think if they never play in a game, then they won't be missed, but their decision can also change the dynamics of a team. The very next year, a bench player who played various roles on our team quit very early on in the season. His departure had just as significant an effect as our starting shooting guard quitting the year before, but it was in a different manner. His absence was felt more in practice. Because he was gone, we had fewer players to compete in the post and our bigger guards had to rotate to that position to fill the void. Then we had to fill in again at the guard position and suddenly players were forced to practice at several different positions that they would normally not play.

We never fully had the time or the proper simulation we needed to get ready for our opponents because of it. Especially since we were a younger team, not only did we need as many repetitions as we could get to be ready for our next game, but we also needed them so we could improve as individuals. This did not help us on the court and it was one of the reasons we struggled that season. Also, because some of the players on our team maintained a friendship with that player they were subjected to the negative comments and ideas that led to the decision for him to quit. These friends also took on resentment for the coaching staff and it created even more negativity in our team dynamics. That one less bench player quitting may not seem like a big deal, but it can be paramount to a team's success and mental health.

Don't Quit Mentally

There is another way to quit on a team without physically separating yourself from it. I have seen plenty of players who don't quit, but begrudgingly stick with their commitment through extreme unhappiness because they do not want to be considered a "quitter." But these players are not doing any kind of good for the team if they have already decided to quit mentally. These players can be spotted very easily by several different signs. They don't give their all in practice, or have bad body language, or even can badmouth the coaches and their teammates, just to name a few. If this is how you are going to act, then there is no question you should physically leave your team. If you are not mentally tough enough to get over your individual problems and focus on helping the team no matter what your role is, then quitting is your best option. I am a firm believer that when a player like this physically quits, then you will have addition by subtraction for your team. But if you can turn your attitude around, remain positive in thought and action by focusing on improving every day and helping your team in any way possible, then you and your team will have much more success. It is not always easy to do this, but the benefits of being in this role far outweigh the negative consequences of quitting.

Conclusion

Both of the players I used as examples of players who quit our team later came back to our practices in the years that followed and deeply regretted the decision they made to physically and mentally quit. They had realized that they not only quit on themselves and their teammates, but they gave up the only chance in their lives where they could be basketball players. Other players who left our team in the off-season, because they felt they were too talented for our team or thought they would be better off in a different situation, never ended up playing at the same level again.

People quit when things do not go their way and they are always looking to find an easier way to success, but the truth is that no matter where you go, you will have to earn your success with hard work, perseverance and toughness. If you decide to give it your all and stand up to your challenges with a "never quit attitude," you will be a better player, person and teammate. No matter how low and lonely you may feel, you can have tremendous value to your team if you stay positive and stick with it. If you want a bigger role, then follow the advice in this book, but realize that nothing is going to be handed to you, you have to work for it. Being a part of a team is not always easy, but nothing worth doing usually is.

Tips for Success

- If you are not happy in your situation you must realize the high costs quitting will have on your team and your future.

- Quitting can come in two different forms. It can be physically removing yourself from your team or giving up mentally.

- You only get so many chances in life to be a part of a competitive team. Do not waste these moments by being selfish and only thinking of yourself.

- There is great value in being a positive player and person no matter the circumstances.

- Quitting is the easy way out. Any one who has ever become their best as a player, teammate and person will tell you it was not easy to accomplish this feat.

Consistency

To get off the bench you have to show your coach consistency. This is what every coach is looking for; they need to know what they are going to get from a player when they are inserted into the game. Being consistent with your play is the key to becoming someone your coach can depend upon and it leads to more minutes and production. Showing consistency is an opportunity you have every day at practice. Anybody can have a great performance one time, but that doesn't mean they are a great player or deserve to play more; it has to be done on a regular basis. Being consistent with any aspect of the game can be hard to do because of the many different challenges you face during the course of a season, but it is the only way you will find yourself playing a bigger role for your team.

In basketball, just like in life, there will be days where you feel good and days you feel bad. You will have days in the gym where you feel like you can't miss and others where nothing seems to go in the basket. Through this you have to be on a continuous quest for consistency as a player. You want to show more good than bad and prove to your coach every time you are in the gym that you can make something positive happen on a consistent basis. By putting in extra work outside of practice (pg. 17), you will, without a doubt, be on your way to being more consistent on the court. However, the skill development necessary may take some time and there is very little that even the best players in the world can make happen 100 percent of the time they are on the court. But there are two things every coach loves to see consistently, and every individual player, no matter what the circumstances, can completely control. If you want to earn more minutes and improve your game, then you must first learn to focus on your effort and attitude, because they are the only variables in sports that can be controlled 100 percent of the time.

Players get too caught up with such things as a coach's substitution pattern, how their teammates aren't passing them the ball or what a terrible call the referee just made. Any of these factors, and many others just like it, can lead to wasted energy and emotion over things that you have little power over changing. If you instead focus on giving your best effort and having a good attitude, you will suddenly be a more productive player. You will be of more value to your teammates and coaches and you will always be a positive person to be around.

This idea, which I have come to know as "controlling the controllables," was first introduced to me by my high school coach. It is all about focusing on what each individual can control so they do not waste any of their time getting caught up with issues that will result in distractions for individuals and a team. So many variables change throughout the course of a basketball game and season, and you need to be able to have positive reactions to them. With a great effort and attitude, this will always be achieved.

Control the Controllables

The years I spent on the bench, when I wasn't showing enough consistency with my skills in practice to get minutes in the game, there were times I got on the court because of my effort and attitude. There were moments that the players who were playing in front of me struggled, the team was not playing hard enough or we just needed a boost of energy. When those moments occurred, it was my name our coach called. He may not have been quite sure what he was going to get from me with my offensive or defensive skills, but he knew I would play my hardest and have a great attitude no matter how well or how long I played. These times led to a few minutes here and there, but more importantly, it gave me an opportunity to play in situations that I had previously not experienced.

This approach also helped me improve because I was not only trying my hardest, but because I was still being coached. My coaching staff talked to me about my development and wanted me to get better. Believe it or not, this can be a rare occurrence for a player who is on the end of the bench, especially if they have a poor attitude. If a player has a bad attitude and does not give a great effort, then they are no fun to coach, especially if they are not as talented as the other players on the team. Also, if a coach looks down the bench to consider putting a player in the game and that player has poor body language or seems to be upset for any personal reason, then there is almost a 100 percent guarantee they will stay on the bench. In both of these cases, it can lead to coaches not even bothering to waste their time working with and helping the player. So I made sure that I gave myself every opportunity to improve my game and become more consistent; I wanted and needed to be coached. This all started every day I went to the gym, with my focus on "controlling the controllables."

Consistency Starts in Practice

A few weeks into my freshman season of basketball, my second year at Sonoma State, I knew it would take some time before I would be able to contribute consistently in game situations. As the season continued on toward the halfway point, it turned out my role was indeed on the bench, but I was still looking for an opportunity to play meaningful minutes. I wanted to show the coaching staff that I could contribute on the court, so the first thing I had to do was show them I could contribute in practice. I had to give my best effort every day and no matter what the circumstances were, I had to have a positive attitude about my role on the team.

I wanted to stand out and I knew it would not be my athleticism, speed or even skills that would help me do this consistently at that time. I had to focus on my effort and attitude, which was hard to keep positive when I was still on the bench. After all, every player wants to be rewarded with minutes and a chance to show what they can do in a game. I knew the value of hard work and that it would eventually pay off for me, but I had to be realistic, even if that meant trying to become a great practice player that year. I had been in a similar role the year before this as well, but now, since I was in my second year, it had been two years since I had seen any real game action. Despite this, the attitude and effort I brought every day allowed me to get better as a player, and finally I got my first real opportunity to play half way through the year.

Effort and Attitude Drive Your Performance

At the afternoon shoot around on Friday, my coach told me I needed to be ready to play because our back-up point guard got into some trouble and was benched for the night. At that point it didn't matter to me how my chance came about, I just wanted to make sure I capitalized on the opportunity. However, with very few chances so far in my whole college career (I had only appeared in five games, and those were just "garbage minutes"), no one knew how it was going to turn out.

This was my first real game action in two years, yet despite that, I ended up playing just as successfully as I had in high school. In my back up role I scored 16 points in 15 minutes, including five assists and only one turnover. The fans went crazy in the stands, as no one expected such output from a player no one had ever really seen play before. One fan even joked with me after the game that all season he thought I was the towel boy. To top off my surprising night, it was the only game that year that was televised, and I was chosen for the post-game interview. I was feeling pretty good about myself, I felt like I had earned some credibility as a college basketball player and, more importantly, I thought I had made a great impression on my head coach. Surely this was the beginning of an increased role on the team.

The very next night, reality struck me hard. Our back-up point guard had returned to the line-up after his one game suspension and that combined with a very athletic opponent made it hard for my coach to find minutes for me. At least, that's what I came up with in my head. Why else would a coach not play a guy who scored so proficiently the night before? So many different thoughts ran through my mind and it all led to me being very upset. In fact, I played a total of three minutes that night and watched as we went on to squeak out a win in overtime. From my standpoint, it was great that we won, but my minutes were tough to swallow after such a solid performance the night before. Had I played, I felt like we would have won the game in regulation because I could have produced just as I did in the previous game. I was letting factors outside of my control affect me in a negative way at that point. Because my thoughts were negative, my attitude became negative as well, and it affected me for the next few days.

My poor attitude over my playing time on Saturday night caused my performance in practice to suffer. It was obvious that I wasn't the same person that week because of my bad attitude. Consequently, my effort was now at an all-time low too. Everything we did in practice seemed to be a waste of time to me; I felt like it didn't matter how well I performed because I wouldn't play anyway. That led to some of the lowest moments of my playing career. I was not being a productive player, teammate or person that week because I let my concerns over my personal playing time become the center of all my thoughts.

It took me a few days to get over my negative feelings, and I decided from that point on, I was not going to let that affect me anymore. I was going to only focus my energy on the factors over which I had complete control, my effort and attitude, because only then would I continue to improve to my highest level of ability. By changing my concentration from being upset with my playing time to giving my best effort and staying positive, I got back in the groove and kept improving as a player every day that year. On those few days when I felt down, I did not improve. They were chances to get better that I missed out on because I was being immature and selfish with my attitude.

The rest of that season, with the exception of our game at UC Davis (more on this later), I would continue with only playing in the last few minutes of already decided games or not playing at all. I had to force myself to worry only about controlling the controllables or I would have gone crazy trying to figure out why I wasn't getting any playing time. My focus kept me in the right mindset and approach toward practice every day. The approach that I took as a freshman would prove invaluable to me throughout the rest of my career, as it would not be until I was a junior that I would get consistent minutes and be a contributor on the court. Because I focused on what I could control, I became a better player every day, even as a young bench player, and it helped me on my journey to becoming my best on the court.

Conclusion

As a player on the bench, you may not have shown enough consistency to your coach and therefore you do not get much playing time. Think about it from a coach's perspective; to put you in the game he has to believe that you will do something to help the team on the court. Where would he get this idea? He sees it in practice. Obviously, if you aren't getting the minutes that you desire there is more you need to show your coach, you have to prove that they should be playing you. By focusing on your effort and attitude, your coach will have no choice but to take notice of the consistency and positivity you bring to the gym. They may not recognize it the first day or even the second, but I guarantee with your best effort and positive attitude spread out over the course of even a month or two, everyone will take notice. In the story I just shared, I had one great night, but that was followed by a bad week of practice, which showed my coaching staff zero consistency. Because of that, I was right back where I started, sitting on the bench. It was a lesson that was hard to learn, but I made sure it was a lesson that I only had to learn once.

Tips for Success

- Players are constantly judged by what they can consistently accomplish on the court.

- For your coach to put you in the game they need to know what you are going to make happen on a consistent basis. The greatest showcase for this is in practice.

- "Controlling the controllables" is about focusing on your effort and attitude, because they are the only two factors that you always have complete control over.

- A positive attitude and great effort are two traits that lead to success on and off the court.

Handle Outside Influences

Over the course of your time as a player you are going to have many different people who will try to have an influence on you. They will give you advice on what they think is necessary for you to become your best on the court and reach the highest levels of play. Everyone from coaches, teammates, family, friends, fans, your next-door neighbor and complete strangers will have an opinion on what you should be doing more of on the basketball court. It is up to you to decide which voices are the ones you should be listening to and which people should be ignored. You always have to consider the source and perspective of each person offering their advice and determine who you should let have an influence on your life.

Dealing with outside influences as a basketball player can be confusing, as some people may be telling you two completely opposite actions for you to take to be more effective. Your coach may be telling you he wants you to drive the ball to the basket more or make the extra pass, while your best friend thinks you should look to shoot from the three point line more often. Your mom or dad may be telling you that you should be playing more during games while your coach is telling you that your play in practice has to get better or you will not be playing at all. With all of the people offering you basketball advice, it can be hard to decide who are the most important to be listening to.

The best advice always comes from the ones who see you in practice every day. Your teammates and coaches are insiders, they know what you consistently provide the team as a player because they see you play in practice every day. They have an understanding of how you fit into the team's system and what you can do differently on the court so your team can achieve a higher level of play. Other people are outsiders; they only see what you do on the court during game situations, which is only a small percentage of what you do for a team. They have no idea what the game plan is for your team and what you have been working on in practice to improve. They want for you to be more successful instead of looking at how you can fit into a role that will make your team better. Anyone outside of your teammates and coaches are outside influences and they typically give you a totally different and selfish view of your role on your team. How you handle these influences will have a major impact on your development as a player and teammate.

Outsiders Have a Distorted View

"Why don't you play more?" "Your coach is an idiot for not playing you." "You're so much better than the player in front of you." "You should be starting." "Why don't you look to shoot the ball more?" "Why did you get subbed out so quickly?" "Why didn't you take the last shot?" "You should transfer." This list could go on for quite a few more pages. These are some examples of very common and negative things outsiders can tell a player and I know because I have either heard these said directly to me or to one of my teammates. None of these comments are constructive for anyone, and all of them are colored by the outsider's feelings for the individual player. These are phrases used to try to make the player feel better about themselves and with them is little regard for the betterment of the team. All of the focus is on the individual.

The biggest problem with an outsider's view, especially when they are a relative or friend, is that when you are in a game these people have tunnel vision, they watch just you almost all of the time. Go to a game sometime and watch the fans in the stands. You will be able to pick out which player is the son or daughter of the fans quite easily by their reactions and what they are watching during certain parts of the game. I didn't realize this phenomenon until my playing career was over and I sat in the stands at youth, high school and even some college games and watched this unfold. How can these same people possibly know what else is going on in the game if they are only watching you? Sometimes when you are subbed out of the game they may even stop paying attention to what is going on in the actual game. Once you see this happen, you will recognize that any person who does this cannot give an impartial opinion because they are only looking out for you and your success. They do not have a clear view of what the bigger team picture looks like.

Now, I am not telling you that you should completely tune out people outside your basketball team when they try to talk to you about your game. I think parents, relatives and friends can have many positive ways of encouraging and helping you. After all, they probably know you better than anyone else. But encouragement is different than giving advice on how many minutes you should be playing and speaking negatively about your coaches and teammates. You need to filter the information from outsiders; an old coach of yours who knows your game might notice something about the way your shooting form looks or one of your parents may have some great advice about your body language on the court. Ultimately, you need to decide if it is valid information, but no matter how great it may be, you cannot let it override the voices of your teammates and coaches.

You Have to Properly Manage Outsiders

I was pretty lucky by the time I got to college because though my parents had watched a lot of basketball, neither of them pretended to be an expert. Sure, my mom had a few negative things to say about my coach every now and then, but I let them go in one ear and out the other. It was a way for her to let off a little steam about my limited playing time, so I simply ignored it. By doing this, I did not encourage these comments because I did not even acknowledge them with dialogue. They never entered my mind as a valid statement because she was upset for me, it didn't have anything to do with how I could improve. My parents usually gave me the best advice after games when I didn't play much (sometimes I didn't play at all), when they kept it short: "Son, just keep working hard." I had no intentions of wanting to rehash a game I might not have played in by analyzing why I didn't play. I was happy to talk about what occurred on the court, but wasn't interested in discussing my personal feelings about my playing time. I think this also helped discourage any negative talk about my teammates or coaches and limited any future conversations about it.

I knew my parents were disappointed for me. They knew it was painful for me not to play, but there was nothing positive that would have come out of putting my teammates or coaches down simply to try and make me feel better. They had seen the success I had when I was a player in high school, as I was always one of the best players on the court, but this was a different level. There was much more I needed to do to get off the bench and play any kind of meaningful minutes.

Besides my parents, I also had to deal with other outsiders who told me I should be playing more. Some even went as far as saying that I was better than some of the starters. I did appreciate their kind words, but I didn't give them much value because they weren't in practice every day. They didn't see the starters kick my butt most of the time or see me get beat on defense on countless occasions. Because I stuck with the things my coaches and teammates had to say as the most valuable, I became a better player and was a great teammate. I earned more minutes on the court because I was working on what I was told was important by my coaching staff. If I had listened to what other people were saying, it could have put mixed ideas in my head and caused my attitude to become negative. I could have had a lot of resentment for my coach, too, because after all, according to the outsiders, it was his fault I wasn't playing. But I didn't let those negative influences have an effect on me. Instead, I listened to the voices that mattered the most. I listened to the voices of the insiders.

Conclusion

With so many people trying to tell you what is best for you, it is up to you to decide who you are going to listen to. It may seem like everyone has your best interests in mind, but that is not always what is in the best interests of your team. By limiting outside influences you will be more focused on your team and individual goals that are laid out by your coaches, teammates and yourself. If every player on a team took this focus, then everyone would be working together toward a shared vision and the benefit would be increased success for the team and each individual. It is usually when distractions from outsiders come into play that tensions and problems occur. If you want to be your best, then filter outside influences and listen to what the insiders say. Their words are the most valid and will lead to increased productivity.

Tips for Success

- You must manage the effect that outsiders have on you regarding your view of yourself and your team.

- *Insiders* (coaches and teammates) see you in practice everyday and have a clear understanding of how you fit into your team's hierarchy and game plan.

- *Outsiders* (parents, friends, relatives, etc.) will often have a distorted view of reality. They will sometimes put others down to make you feel better. Their view focuses on your feelings and what they think is best for you, not what is always best for your team.

- Make sure your group of outsiders are positive and supportive individuals, and that you value the opinions of your teammates and coaches above all others.

Responsibility Off the Court

When you are on a team, you are a member of a group committed to a cause greater than your individual self. With that membership comes a responsibility that you have to your teammates and coaches to become your best on the court. But more importantly, you have a duty to become even greater off the court. Many players do not realize that the actions they take and the decisions they make outside the gym have an impact on their performance in the gym. To reach your highest level of play, you have to have your life in order, and you have to find the proper balance between basketball and your personal affairs. The easiest way to ensure this success is to know your priorities and manage your time properly.

It must never be forgotten that everywhere you go, you represent yourself, your teammates, coaches, family, athletic department, school and surrounding community. Any decision you make, either positive or negative, is an example to others about who you are and those you represent. You may be the only exposure an outsider will ever have to someone from your team, so it is your duty to make sure that they always leave with a positive impression.

Be Self-Disciplined

In all situations off the court you have to be responsible for yourself by being self-disciplined and using self-control. You do not want to jeopardize your performance on the court by losing focus off the court. Situations that can lead to losing focus include staying up too late, surrounding yourself with people who might be a negative influence and partaking in activities that include drugs and alcohol. You may have to give up some of the things other people your age are doing, sacrificing that time so you can be fully prepared both mentally and physically for your next game or practice. You won't be able to go to that late night movie or the party on Friday night, but you will be better on the court for having made that sacrifice.

You are accountable to your teammates and coaches for your choices, so it is imperative that you make the right decisions; they should be ones that will not result in any kind of negative consequences. You have to make sure that you are always contributing at your highest level and staying focused on the things that really matter in a season. When you lose focus of what is important, then off the court, mistakes will happen. You can make your decisions off the court easier by prioritizing what is important in your life. You only get so many opportunities to play competitive sports, do not waste these moments by not knowing where you should be placing your focus and energy.

Prioritize Your Life

My college coach always told us if we want to be responsible team members, our priorities should be in this order: 1. Religion/Spirituality 2. Family 3. School 4. Basketball 5. Friends/Social Activities. It can be difficult as a young person to have to put your friends last, especially when you may see the freedom and fun that some of them are having. But being on a team is about making sacrifices and this list correctly places the order for someone who is a fully committed teammate. Your religion, family and school are the only things that come before your sport and even those have to be managed properly because of your commitment to your team.

School

School is ahead of basketball on the list of priorities because you should be a student first and an athlete second. Your responsibility to your team in regards to school means managing your time so you always get your school work completed. Do not use school as an excuse to miss any time on the court because you procrastinated and put your work off until the last minute. This means it is essential that you complete your assignments and ensure they are of the highest quality. Nothing good comes out of speeding through any task at the last minute and producing low quality work.

Once you find that balance between basketball and school, and learn to manage your time, then you will flourish and soon realize there is nothing more valuable than an education. When I graduated from Sonoma State University, I left more satisfied with the knowledge I had acquired in the classroom than any basketball experience I ever had. The thoughts and ideas I was exposed to opened my eyes to new ways of viewing the world. To this day I am on a constant quest to satisfy my thirst for learning and knowledge that was fueled by my time as a student in the classroom. This need to continually keep learning has made me a better person in society by causing me to frequently question the world around me and look for ways to improve my life.

In the years since my basketball career has ended, I have realized what an educational opportunity that basketball really was. Through my sport I was taught many lessons on perseverance, hard work and commitment. Basketball even took me halfway across the world to Vienna, Austria, where I played after college. Living in a foreign country was the ultimate learning experience, as I had to adjust to life in a different culture and society. The combination of classroom and athletic education I received are invaluable, but I would have never completed this educational journey without taking responsibility for myself off the court and managing my time properly.

You have to remember that completing your work in the classroom is just as important as your play in the gym. The two go hand in hand, because if you do not take care of business in the classroom, then your basketball will suffer. I have seen players who become distracted because of a big test that is approaching or an assignment that needs to be done at the last minute. The ultimate failure in the classroom is performing low enough so you become academically ineligible. When this happens it can be hard to recover from and it has a huge effect on everyone involved with your team. Your teammates and coaches count on you to do your work in the classroom and if you do not make this a priority, then you are not only letting yourself down, but you are also letting your team down. You should not take for granted the opportunities you have to compete in your sport and gain an education. If you are not responsible and cannot learn to balance the two, then both can be taken away from you very quickly.

Family

Family is a very important aspect of everyone's lives, but it is a priority that needs to be properly managed to ensure an equal balance in your life. I played competitive basketball from the third grade to professional and while family has always been more important to me than basketball, I did have to sacrifice time with my family, especially during the holidays. Basketball is a winter sport, so when I got to college I missed a few Thanksgivings and other family gatherings because we had a game, practice or other team function. This did not happen often, but it was a sacrifice that was necessary to make for my team. It was all part of the balance I had to have in my life so I could be a committed and responsible team member.

While this section on family is short, it needs to be noted that there is no other priority higher than family, except of course for religion. But family obligations and pressures can lead to distractions if you and your family do not understand that sacrifices are going to need to be made for you to be able to balance all of your priorities.

Religion/Spirituality

Religion/Spirituality is number one on the list and it can be a huge advantage if utilized. There is a definite benefit to having some kind of spiritual connection. My spiritual connection comes from my background in the Lutheran Church. I grew up attending Gloria Dei Lutheran Church and School, where the connection I felt to God through His lessons in the Bible are ones I will forever have in my heart and mind. I used this as a source of motivation and strength in my everyday life as an athlete. Every morning I woke up, I used a verse or story from one of the four gospels in the New Testament as encouragement. I then took time to be thankful to have another opportunity to be alive and have a chance to play and practice a game I love. This approach ensured that I used every day I had to its fullest and therefore I became a better player for having this mindset and spirituality.

For others it may be a spiritual connection through nature or another religion, but whatever it is, you should focus on it and work on developing it so you can grow as an individual. There is a certain inner peace and strength that comes with finding this connection and it can have everlasting effects on your life. It is all part of the balance between your priorities that needs to occur and it is an essential piece to taking care of yourself and becoming your best.

All of these priorities are undoubtedly ones that in one way or another are a part of your life. You have to handle being part of a team by figuring out where your priorities lie and finding the necessary balance between them. By focusing on what is truly important and being a responsible person, you will only see improvement in yourself. When I played, the only time we ran into off the court problems was when the players on our team lost track of their priorities. There were instances where my teammates did not go to class, did not complete assignments and they ended up being ineligible academically. Guys on my team also went out to party and hang out with their friends at the wrong time, such as on nights when we had an early morning practice or a game the next day. Obviously this hurt their performance on the court and it affected everyone on our team negatively. These are all situations you will want to aviod if you are truly committed to being a responsible teammate on and off the court.

Conclusion

When you do not take responsibility for yourself off the court, you will have to deal with the consequences, and those consequences have an effect on more than just you. It is up to you to realize how important it is to be a good teammate, which does not stop once you step outside of the gym. You will have to make sacrifices off the court for your team to ensure that you are always performing at your highest level. Figure out the balance needed in your priorities and what needs to be changed so you can be more successful in every aspect of your life. It will be a lesson on responsibility that will guide you in your journey to improving now and into the future.

Tips for Success

- The actions you take and the decisions you make outside the gym will have an impact on your performance in the gym.

- You may have to give up some of the things other people your age are doing, sacrificing that time so you can be fully prepared both mentally and physically for your next game or practice.

- Your spirituality, family and school are the only things that come before your sport and even those have to be managed properly to be a fully committed and responsible team member.

Utilize Every Opportunity

Every chance you get on the court is an opportunity to improve your status on the team. It is a chance to prove to yourself, your coaches and your teammates that you can be a regular contributor on the court. There are two very crucial times that are your chances to prove your worth as a player: practices and games. But before you can successfully perform physically on the court during these times, you have to approach them with the right mindset. You have to stay mentally ready at all times so you can be sure to be ready to perform at your highest level physically. Letting any opportunity pass, no matter how big or small, is a huge mistake because it is your chance to prove you belong on the court.

Practice is Your Biggest Opportunity

Practice is the biggest showcase for a player to demonstrate that they can consistently play effectively and understand the concepts that the coach is teaching. It is a pretty standard belief in basketball that you will play like you practice, so if you aren't very good during practice, then the chances are you won't be very good during the game. If you are not in the rotation on game day, practice becomes even more important for you. Instead of viewing practice as the time you get ready for games, you have to treat every practice like it is your game. This is your chance to compete with the players who are playing instead of you, to show that you can play with them and even beat them. By improving your performance in practice, you will get more chances in game situations. You cannot be a bad practice player and think you will suddenly get increased game time; you have to start by earning that time.

This perspective will not only make you a better player, but it will make your teammates better because of the challenge you are giving them. This is good for everybody on the team; it is the closest thing you have to simulating a game situation. It prepares your teammates for the intensity that they will see from your opponents. If even one of your teammates does not rise to the occasion and compete with you on an everyday basis, they will lose their spot. It should be your goal to take their spot from them. If you do not accomplish this feat, you will at least know that they earned it because you made them work for it.

This can be a hard viewpoint to take and it can take some time before you see any change in your status on your team. But you have no other choice; if you don't play in the games, this is your opportunity to prove that you should be. Every drill, scrimmage and competition is your chance to compete with the players who get the minutes on game day, so it is imperative that you push yourself to a higher level.

Practice is Your Game

During my sophomore season, I was in the situation where I had to treat practice like it was my game. It's not that I didn't go as hard as I could in practice before this, but I looked at every part of practice a bit differently. With only one senior on our team, we were young, inexperienced and struggling to win games. In order to prove to my coach that I belonged on the court, I went into every practice with the goal of outworking everyone in the gym and winning every competition. If I wasn't going to play, then the players in front of me were going to have to earn their minutes. When other players might have had the chance to possibly "coast" through a practice, I had to try and take advantage of it. I had to utilize every second I was on the court.

What was even harder for me during this season was that our team did not get positive results in our games. I was forced to watch as we got beaten two out of every three games we played during the first half of the season, which was made worse by the fact that we lost seven in a row early in the year. In practice our second string was so bad we lost almost every scrimmage and competition drill against the first group. Although our second group did not win much, we continued to work as hard as we could so we could challenge the first team. We started acting like practice was our game and suddenly it felt like we wanted to win more than we had before. With that mentality, something began to happen as the season went into its final month. We were getting better as a team and I was improving dramatically. My practice intensity had paid off and I started to see the results in most drills and scrimmages. I wasn't winning every drill or match-up with my teammates, but I was performing at a level where I had never been before. I was making any player who went against me better because I challenged them with my best effort, which in turn improved every day.

This all led to an increase of just a few minutes of game action. That is something some players might laugh at, but it was time I wasn't getting before. Eventually this effort carried into the next year where I started contributing off the bench consistently during the second half of the season and it prepared me for my senior year when I became the starting point guard. Without the effort I put into practice when I was younger, I would not have been close to the player I became later on. I was ready for the game situations I was put into because I treated every practice with the same importance others do with a game. I had to make sure I didn't let this opportunity pass me by.

Always Be Ready

You never know when you're going to get your chance to go in the game. It is no longer a practice situation. If you forget one minor detail, like correct defensive positioning or how to execute a certain play, your coach cannot blow a whistle and tell you to go back and try it again. Now every second matters, one mental or physical mistake can be the difference in the game and your team's season. It is another chance to show your coach you can contribute when you are called upon. It may start as a minute or two, but if you do something positive during those times, it can lead to even more opportunities. That is why it is so important that any chance you get to play in a game, you enter it aware of what is happening on the court. You have to stay in the game mentally when you are on the bench, even if you think you have no chance to play in the game physically.

Many players "check out" of the game in their head when they are sitting on the bench. Examples can be players talking about non-basketball matters or staring into the stands, looking to see who's in the crowd. It can be a form of passive resistance to their situation, almost saying, "Why should I care? I'm not going to play." As a bench player and a player who wants more minutes, you have to earn them. Besides practice, the best way to do this is to prove that you belong on the floor when you go into the game. You have to realize that every opportunity you receive as a player, especially in a game situation, is your chance to show that you belong on the court. You do not want to miss your chance to impress because you were not paying attention, because you were mentally "checked out."

In order to stay mentally "checked in" while on the bench, you have to get in the huddle during timeouts and listen to what the coaches are saying and the feedback the players on the court are giving. Watch the game with a critical eye, see what offenses and defenses are the most effective. Try to spot some tendencies of the players on the other team and watch your teammates and notice who is playing well and who is not. All of this will keep your mind in the game and away from your own potentially negative thoughts. It will make you a more effective player and when you get the call to go in the game, you will know the situation and be ready to help your team immediately.

Stay in the Game Mentally

When I was a freshman I got the surprise of my career when our coach had me finish one of the biggest games of our season on the court. It was my homecoming game, as we were playing on the road at UC Davis, who was also one of our top conference rivals. Since I had decided to go to college in the North Bay Area of California, it meant that every time we traveled to UC Davis, I would be playing in front of all my friends and family. Davis, California lies just twenty minutes outside of my hometown of Sacramento, and the most important people in my life would be there for the first time to watch me play as a college basketball player. The only problem is that since it was my freshman season, there was little to no chance that I would be actually playing in the game.

It was hard not to be a little embarrassed because the people who really mattered to me, everyone who would be there that night, had watched me succeed on the basketball court my whole life. I forced myself to block out these thoughts because they would be distractions from what I needed to do to stay in the game mentally while I was on the bench. It is what I had to do if I was going to be effective, if for some odd reason that night I actually got called on to play. Feeling sorry for myself would not help me if I went in the game, nor would it be productive even if I didn't play that night.

When the game got underway and then went into halftime, it turned out that I was, in fact, relegated to waving my towel and cheering on my teammates from the bench. All the thoughts and feelings I had about wanting to play in front of my friends and family were in the back of my mind. I would catch myself peeking up to the second level where they were sitting and it took all my mental strength to forget about it and focus on what was happening on the court.

As the game grew into the late moments of the second half, I had been sitting for more than 35 minutes of game time, which was the equivalent of about an hour and a half of actual time. Everything was going against the possibility of me playing on this particular night. Since the score was tied, there would be no way I would be stepping on the floor since I hadn't played in one game that season when the score was within ten points. I had been on the bench for so long and not in the rotation at all that year, so all of my basketball knowledge told me this would not be my time. Then something strange happened. With a little over four minutes to go, everything changed. For some odd reason I thought I heard my coach tell me to go check in the game.

Our head coach, who had a quick temper and, when he got angry, an even quicker substitution pattern, took our starting point guard out of the game after a bad turnover. Then the backup point guard went into the game and made another bad play. At this point, when keeping possession of the ball and executing our half court offense meant everything to our success, he told me to go in!

I couldn't believe it, why in the world would he be putting me in now? Was he crazy? Of course, not all of this really registered in my head until after the game, because before he could finish his sentence I had my warm up off and I was at the scorers table. I was eagerly waiting for a dead ball so I could get on the court and prevent my coach from changing his mind and telling me to come back to the bench. Though the game was close, I wasn't at all scared and, in fact, I was excited to finally get the chance to help my team win a close game.

It was now up to me to run our team. After watching the last two point guards get the quick yank out of the game, it was anybody's best guess how long my time on the court would actually last before I became a victim of the substitution carousel. Like all the other distractions that night, I had to block it out. I just had to focus on what was happening on the court at that moment.

Since I had been into the game mentally all night on the bench, I knew exactly what was going on. I knew our opponents were playing a 2-3-zone defense. I knew exactly what our coach wanted to see from us offensively and defensively because I was paying attention during timeouts and listening to his instructions. I knew which plays had been the most effective all night and, most importantly, I knew which of my teammates were playing particularly well. I knew which player I would be defending on the other team and some of their tendencies. I had done all I could to stay mentally checked into the game without being on the floor. I did it all because, despite the slim odds of me playing, I knew I needed to be ready if my opportunity came.

The first three minutes I was in, baskets were scored fairly consistently back and forth for both teams, keeping the game tied and helping me stay on the court. I had passed the ball inside a few times to our center to get some good looks, but I had also missed a three point attempt. With less than a minute to go, and the game still tied, I found that I had the ball in my hands with the shot clock running down. I dribbled around a high on-ball screen at the top of the key and got to the free throw line area where I picked up my dribble. I was going to make a pass down to our center on the block, but the passing lane closed quickly. But I had been watching that passing lane close all night from the bench so I was prepared to shoot a fifteen-foot jumper. With just two seconds on the shot clock, I put up the shot over the outstretched hand of the defender and watched as the ball went straight through the net as the shot clock buzzer sounded. I will never forget the sound of the hushed and stunned crowd and the ecstatic cheers that came from my teammates on the bench and from the section of the gym where my friends and family were sitting. I had made what turned out to be the game winner. A player who had played in three games all season up to that point and sat the bench for all but the last four minutes of the game had decided the outcome. It was an unbelievable feeling; it was a night I will always remember.

It all happened because, despite the grim outlook earlier in the game, I kept my mind focused and I was into the game mentally. I put all my negative thoughts aside and focused my energy on encouraging my teammates and thinking about the game critically. I was into the game mentally because I had involved myself in timeouts, I had watched the game and analyzed it and I knew exactly the situation when I checked in. Now there were many times that year when that focus and energy didn't matter as much as they did this night because I didn't get the call to go in the game. But I knew I had to stay ready because I wasn't sure when my time might come, but if I wanted to be effective when I went in, I had to be mentally in the game. That is the role of a bench player. Even if you are the last player on the bench, you have to be in the game mentally.

At the end of the regular season that year, our team ended up getting an at-large berth to the Division II NCAA tournament. We were the seventh seed out of eight teams in the west region, and if we had lost one more game, we might not have made the tournament at all. If we had not won that game at UC Davis, our season may have ended prematurely. It made me realize how important always staying ready by being into the game mentally is for every player and the effect everyone, from the best player to the last man on the bench, can have on the outcome of a game and a season.

Conclusion

As a bench player, you will get opportunities to show what you can do. Whether that opportunity is in a game situation, by playing half the game or just a few seconds, or in practice, you have to show you are capable of making a contribution. When this happens, you will increase your coach's confidence in you and it will lead to more chances on the court. Do not let yourself get distracted by negative thoughts or feelings, instead utilize every opportunity you have. During games "check in" to the game mentally, and make sure you are ready to perform when you are called upon. These game situations, and every day at practice, are opportunities that you must take full advantage of if you want to have increased value on your team.

Tips for Success

- Every second you are on the court, during practices, games, and workouts, is an opportunity to improve your game and status on your team.

- Practice is the biggest and best opportunity to prove that you should be playing in game situations.

- Practice must be approached with the same urgency as games. If you take this mindset you and your team will be stronger.

- You have to be ready at all times on game day. Stay mentally checked in to the game so you can perform successfully when you get on the court.

Love the Game

There are times where being a part of a team can mentally and physically drag you down. Going to practice begins to seem like a burden; it is something you may not feel like doing, but you have to go. If you are sitting on the bench and struggling for minutes, it can be especially hard to figure out why you continue to do it. Being a member of a team is a commitment that requires making many different sacrifices and requires a lot of extra energy. To remedy this problem, and any problem you ever face in basketball, there is only one solution that will totally cure your affliction. This solution can be used any time you are faced with a challenge and it will help you overcome anything. The solution is that you have to find your love and passion for the game of basketball.

It is of the utmost importance to find the reasons why you love the game, figure out what drives you and gets you excited about the sport. At some point in your life, you loved playing the game, so what was it that made you love it? If you can find the answer to this question, your whole outlook will change. You will look forward to going to the gym every day and every moment you get to spend with a basketball will be like a breath of fresh air. You will realize how fortunate you are to be a basketball player and to be a member of a team.

Suddenly, the extra time you put into improving your skills and the sacrifices you make in other aspects of your life, won't be a burden, but rather a necessity and a time of pleasure and satisfaction.

It is so important to recognize that you have the power to control how you feel about the game. No one else, not a coach, teammate or opponent, can take away your love for the game. No one can steal from you the passion and excitement that goes along with being a basketball player. Finding your love can make you become such a passionate player that it becomes infectious and it will influence your teammates and coaches as well. Your love and enthusiasm for the game will turn you into a better player and will be an inspiration to those around you.

Find Your Love - The Sacramento Kings

I was always reminded of why I love basketball whenever I watched my favorite NBA team, the Sacramento Kings. Growing up in Sacramento, California, the Kings were the only major sports team in town, and no matter how good or bad they performed on the court, I loved them. They moved to Sacramento in 1985 and struggled for many of those early years. That is, until it all seemed to turn around in 1999. I was a high school sophomore in that 50 game, lockout-shortened season when the Kings acquired a new batch of exciting players. Under their new coach, Rick Adelman, the Kings exhibited a style of play that forever changed how I viewed the game of basketball. Their free flowing offense made me burst at the seams with excitement and I fell in love with their unselfish passing and ball movement. I was mesmerized by their rookie point guard Jason Williams. He was like a magician with the ball, using an assortment of behind the back passes and extremely high-risk plays that showed me a completely different way to play the game.

Throughout the next six years, my love for the game grew stronger with the success of the Kings. I was fortunate enough to witness some of the best basketball in the world during that time, as the Kings made runs to the second round of the playoffs and conference finals. I was in the arena during classic battles with the Lakers, Mavericks and Jazz, and I got to witness the passion and excitement of the Sacramento fans who went absolutely crazy with their love of the way the team played. Every time you went to their stadium, Arco Arena, it was guaranteed to be a sell out crowd and a place where at some point during the game you would not be able to hear yourself think because of the crowd noise. The fans were so eager to watch the Kings play that the arena would be near full capacity twenty minutes before the game when the team came on the court for pre-game warm-ups. I was so excited I wanted to get to the arena ninety minutes before tip-off, which was as soon as the doors opened, so I could watch some of the players do individual pre-game shooting. The whole atmosphere was infectious and anyone in the arena could not help but fall in love with the game every time they were there. It was an exhibition of what love, passion and excitement for the game is all about.

I can still remember moments that took my breath away as a basketball fan. There were the biggest moments for the Kings, like when Mike Bibby beat the Lakers with a mid range jumper in the final seconds to put the Kings up three games to two in the Western Conference Finals. I couldn't even hear my own scream, though I was yelling at the top of my lungs. There was also the moment where the Sacramento fans showed their knowledge and appreciation for basketball history. In 2003, the Kings eliminated the Utah Jazz and I, along with everyone else in the arena, gave a standing ovation for John Stockton and Karl Malone as they exited the floor. Goosebumps covered my whole body because I was watching the end of an era. The greatest one-two combination in all of basketball history was never going to play on the same court again and though our team had suffered for a few years in losses to that same Jazz team, we knew how special that moment was; it was bigger than our team's win. That was one of the truest forms of love and appreciation for the game I have ever witnessed. It is something I will never forget.

There were also many little moments that added up to equal more to me as a basketball player and fan than anyone could have ever known. Times like when reserve Jon Barry came on the court for only two to three minutes of play, but it was enough time for the whole arena, some 17,317 people, to chant his name. His all-out effort on every play showed us how much he loved being on the court and what was so inspiring was how everyone in the arena recognized it and appreciated him for it. On one particular occasion, he dove for a ball on the defensive end of the floor, ended up in the stands and got up to run down the court to nail a three pointer. It was incredible to me because the fans recognized how special his effort was, how he never gave up on a play and was always giving his best no matter how long he was on the court. And it wasn't like he had to take such risks, he did it because he loved to play the game, his passion was evident in his effort. He was only one part of a whole team who showed me what it means to have fun on the court through their love and passion for basketball. Every member of the Kings seemed to cherish their time together. It didn't matter who was playing, you could see their love for the game reflected in their performance. I wanted nothing else than to mimic these players and try to reproduce these feelings for my teammates, coaches and self.

I used the Kings for inspiration, as they served as reminders of why I love the game of basketball; they always brought on feelings of excitement about the game for me. I loved the feeling I got from seeing a pristine pass, a clutch three pointer or a player who was willing to sacrifice his body for the team. I would spend hours on the court pretending I was on the Kings hitting a big three pointer and hearing the crowd erupt. I wasn't afraid to dream of being a great player and becoming like the members of my favorite Kings team. This continued well into college, where I still felt the same joy and excitement I had when I watched the Kings play when I was younger, it produced a special feeling in my heart that I have never lost.

I also used the Kings as motivation before I went to the gym for my own games. I would watch a Kings and Mavericks playoff game from 2002 before every game I played. The Kings won game four of that series in overtime, as Mike Bibby came up with huge baskets in the fourth quarter and overtime. This game gave the Kings ultimate control of the series and they would go on to win game five to win the series four games to one. This game and series got me so inspired and ready to play that I could hardly contain myself hours before tip-off. This also translated to practices where there was very little that could bring me down off my basketball high. Every challenge I faced was met with my excitement and enthusiasm for the game of basketball. Every drill or scrimmage that we participated in was exciting for me. Even when I did not perform well, I used the Kings as motivation and inspiration to keep my fire for the game burning inside of me.

Remember Your Happiest Moments - Driveway Basketball

Before the 1999 Kings, I had begun to see my joy and love for the game develop on my driveway in front of my childhood home. Whenever I was frustrated, I remembered the first moments when I touched a basketball. I would go back to where it all started, where my basketball journey began, with my family and friends playing in our driveway. I still remember the day I was leaving for school and saw my dad, uncle and grandfather pouring concrete and putting in our first ten foot high basketball hoop. From that day forward, I was in love with basketball.

I had so many classic battles with my dad, brother and friends on that court. Most importantly for me, though, was that this was my court, a place where I could be alone and just play basketball because I loved it. I didn't have to live up to anybody else's expectations, and the only rules that mattered were the ones I made up. This court was where I found ultimate peace and happiness; nothing else in the world mattered when I was there. Because of that peacefulness, I spent hours on that court, practicing night after night, lost in my love for the game.

My driveway was also the place where I was first motivated to try to become my best, it was where I was taught how to compete. I played "H-O-R-S-E," "Around the World," "21," "one on one," "two on two," and any other shooting game or competition you can think of that involves a basketball. These were the moments I loved the most because I had nothing else to worry about except being immersed in the game.

These thoughts always encouraged me to remember what a great game basketball is, how I have enjoyed it for so many years in so many different forms. This is truly when I started to love the game and these memories got me through a lot of hard times later in my career as a player. Whenever I felt down, I could always visualize my dad's running hook shot across the lane and my brother and I battling in a one on one game or three-point competition. I could also remember being alone on the court with nothing more than a basketball in my hand and a smile on my face. To this day I would have to say that these memories are the ones I will always cherish. They are more important to me than anything else I accomplished as a basketball player.

Conclusion

Though I found different ways to let my passion and love for the game inspire me, there were still days in the gym that were tough to handle. They became easier to deal with because I found my love, passion and excitement for the game. The daily challenges were so much easier to get past because I loved being in the gym. I embraced the challenges I faced and looked at them as an avenue for improvement. It was very hard for me to get down on myself for too long and my teammates all took notice of how much I enjoyed being a part of our team. As I mentioned in the introduction, through my four years as a player, from being the last player on the bench as a freshman all the way to being an all-conference player as a senior, my teammates voted me the most inspirational player every year. I never intended to have that kind of impact on our team, I just showed up every day feeling excited to be there and loving the opportunity I had to play the game I was passionate about. I was able to inspire others because I knew what inspired me, I knew why I loved the game of basketball.

You can feel this same passion for the game if you can find your inspiration and figure out what makes you love basketball. It may be a positive childhood memory, a coach who pushed you to be your best or, like me, watching your favorite players and teams compete. Whatever it is about this game, you are doing yourself and those around you a disservice if you do not love it. Every day you get to play basketball is a gift and should be treated as such. Find what you are passionate about in the game and you will discover incredible happiness and joy. You will embrace new challenges and the time and commitment you make will become necessary instead of obligatory. You will want to put in more time to becoming a better player and your game will become the best it has ever been.

Tips for Success

- Finding your love and passion for the game will make you a better player and an inspiration to everyone around you.

- Whether it is watching your favorite team play or a positive memory from your past, figuring out what brings you joy in the game will drive you to be your best.

- Love the game. Even the lowest moments for a player, when they are struggling and frustrated, can become a source of internal and external joy by simply loving the game and having a burning passion for it.

Embrace Your Role

Along your journey as a basketball player, you could end up playing several different roles for your team. As a bench player, you may be confused at times, not sure of what that role is because your minutes may vary from one game to another. You may also never get to play; your primary role may be in practice, focusing on helping your teammates prepare for the next game. The one characteristic of a good team, though, is that everyone learns to embrace their role. It may take you some time to figure out what that role is, but once you do, you must not only succeed in it, but learn to thrive in it.

You will never see a good team where five guys on the court demand the ball in their hands. It never works when everyone tries to dominate the ball on offense and there is no attempt to work together. Nor will you see good teams who have players on the bench whose egos cannot handle being in a reserve role. This creates bad chemistry and jealousy among teammates and it leads to a situation where no one is playing the necessary roles to be successful. Every role on a team is important, from team manager to head coach; everyone has a job to do. Without everyone accepting their job within a team, everything turns to chaos and no one can ever reach their potential. For any team to be its strongest it is the duty of every team member to recognize their role and embrace it.

Excel in Every Role

During the five years I was a college player, I played probably every role you can think of on a team. I went from being a redshirt who wasn't allowed to play on game day, to a bench player who never got to play, then a bench player who saw occasional time on the court, followed by a bench player who contributed consistently and finally a starter who played almost the entire game. While I was never the best player on the team while I was in college, I did experience this for a season when I was in high school. With all these roles I played I learned one important lesson: I couldn't get to the next step up on my team without finding a way to succeed in the role I was currently playing. Of course, when I was the player at the end of the bench, I wanted to be a starter, but that wasn't going to happen right away. I had to focus on moving up the depth chart one role at a time.

To succeed in my role I had to have the ability to first recognize what role I was currently playing. It can be hard for any player to do this because you may be confused about what your role is. It is so vital to get a clear definition, and if you need help figuring it out, you should never hesitate to ask one of your coaches. It is so refreshing to get a grasp on what your coach thinks your role is because you will finally be able to focus on excelling in a way that will be beneficial for you and your team.

Once I figured out that my role was the last player on the bench and being used on the court only as a practice player, I did my best to stay positive and focus on how I could excel in that situation. I wanted to be the best "last player on the bench" in the country. My thought was that if I could become an outstanding player on the court, and I was still the last player on our bench, then that would mean we were a very good team. A team is only as strong as their weakest player, so if that player was going to be me, I wanted to make sure I was doing everything possible so we could be a strong team. I did not want to be responsible for holding us back, I wanted to contribute no matter how much playing time I received.

While in this pursuit to excel in my role, I knew that if I became that outstanding last player on the bench and we were not an excellent team, then my chances of getting on the court could only increase. It was the same for every one of the other roles I played, from a consistent contributor off the bench to becoming a starter. I wanted to become the best in every role, thus translating to us being a better and stronger team. Because of this, I challenged the players in front of me and they in turn challenged the players in front of them. We were all better because I learned what it took to excel in every role, which constantly challenged my teammates. The other players had a choice: become better in your role or lose it to me. I did this by developing and following the *BENCH RULES* method. It helped me get from one role to the next, because it was focused on improving every aspect of my game and self. It was not about becoming the best player on my team right away, but the best player I could be in my current role.

The Ultimate Teammate

During my senior year, I became the starting point guard for our team. I had been rewarded with the position because the four previous years I had worked my way up the ladder and succeeded in many different roles. While I was given this opportunity, it meant that one of my teammates had been sent to the bench. He was also a senior and had been the starting point guard for the previous three seasons. Since I had spent that time on the bench, I had watched him grow as a player his whole college basketball career and now he was suddenly forced to sit while I was given his spot. It was a situation where I don't think anyone who hasn't experienced it can even begin to try and describe what he was feeling. I had seen and heard of players on several teams throughout my career who had been put in the same situation and they either quit or became huge problems for their team. My teammate could have taken this path, too, but instead he decided to embrace his new role and help our team in any way he could.

Instead of complaining, pouting or quitting, our starting point guard for the past three years decided to be a contributor in his role on the bench. In practice he never gave anything but his best effort, just as he had his whole career. During games, instead of being on the floor, he used his knowledge and experience from the past three seasons to help his teammates on the sideline and in the huddle. He conversed with the coaching staff on the bench and helped by giving his suggestions on team strategy. He was also still a player who had an impact on the floor during games and late in the year he came off the bench to help lead a furious comeback win for us on the road. At the end of the season we won our conference championship by one game, so it is needless to say we wouldn't have done it without his support. He was a real example of what it means to be a team player and is the greatest teammate I have ever been around. Because of the things he did for our team, he helped us win more games than we could have without him. When all seemed to turn against him on the court, he decided to embrace his role and be a contributor and we were all the better because of it.

The Ultimate Role Player

There was one professional player I always admired because of his willingness to embrace his role and sacrifice his numbers for the betterment of his team. Scottie Pippen played alongside arguably the greatest player of all time and he will be remembered by most basketball fans as Michael Jordan's sidekick. He is a player, who on another team, or in another situation, would have been that team's best player. Instead, he embraced his role as the number two guy on the six-time champion Chicago Bulls and because of it he also became known as one of the best basketball players to ever step on the court.

There was a short two season period where Michael Jordan retired from basketball and Pippen was suddenly the best player on the team who now had the responsibility of being the "go-to-guy." When Jordan came back from his retirement, Pippen made a decision to embrace his role again as being a secondary option to Jordan. It was Pippen who would take on any challenge, including often focusing on shutting down the other team's best player on defense. It is not a role most superstar players would take, after all, using most of your energy on defense doesn't lead to huge numbers in the points or assists column. But what it did was lead to their opponent's best player having limited production and it made a huge contribution to the Bulls' success. From there they went on to win three straight championships for a total of six in eight years.

Both Michael Jordan and Scottie Pippen are hall of famers now and while it may seem easy to embrace your role when you are playing with the best player in NBA history, it can be said that neither would have been as successful without the other. If Pippen had been selfish and unwilling to recognize he needed to defer to Jordan, there could have been major problems for their team and their careers may not have turned out the same. Instead, Pippen embraced and thrived in his role and both he and Jordan became basketball legends. If a hall of fame player like Pippen can learn to embrace his role, and even accept a lesser one in which he sacrificed his numbers for the better of the team, then I believe that anyone can learn to do it.

Conclusion

Every player will benefit from the clarity that comes with knowing where they stand on a team and what needs to be done to contribute to its success. Even professionals who are at the top of the sport have recognized the importance of each player embracing their role so the team can succeed. Once you have learned to embrace your role, you can then start to fully make an impact at your highest level. Too many players get caught up with their statistics and view their success by their total of points, assists or rebounds. Once every player fully understands and embraces their role, your whole team will be on its way to becoming its best. Just one player, no matter how talented, can hold the success of a team back, so it is essential that you do whatever it takes to excel in whatever role it is you play.

Tips for Success

- Every player has a role to play on a team. When these roles are recognized and accepted, then a team will be allowed to reach its full potential.

- It should be your goal to excel in your role, whether it is as a practice player or your team's top scorer.

- To figure out your role you may need some guidance; your coaching staff is the best source for this advice.

- To improve your status on your team you must thrive in your role. You cannot do this without first recognizing what that role is and embracing it.

Support Your Team in Different Ways

It should be the goal of every player to support their team in every way possible. It doesn't matter if you are the most talented player on a team or you are the last man on the bench, you can have a huge impact on your team's success without even scoring a point. Most players judge their contribution by looking at stats and while this is important, there are many other ways to contribute to your team that are equally as crucial. You may not play at all on game day, but you can still make a positive contribution. It takes many different players working toward the same goal to equal success on a team. These contributions can be made in many different ways, including your play in practice, your leadership in the locker room or even your observations from the bench.

As a bench player for my first three years in college, I had a lot of opportunities to make contributions that go beyond statistics. From my redshirt season to my junior year, I did all I could to make our team better without playing a lot in games. I still had moments early on where I got too caught up in the box score at the end of the game and how it read "DNPCD" (Did Not Play, Coaches Decision) by my name. That meant I didn't play because my coach decided not to put me in the game, not because of an injury or some other reasonable excuse. It was then I started to realize that if I was not going to play much in games, I needed to find alternative ways to help make a difference. I wanted to be a contributor to our team and have an effect on the results on game day, even if I didn't play a minute on the court.

Contributing in Practice

While I was a redshirt my first year at Sonoma State, I got to practice with the team, but didn't even get to wear a uniform on the bench during the games. The year was filled with focusing on my individual improvement and helping the team get ready in practice. I did this mainly by playing on the scout team, which was filled with players who were redshirts like myself or who were active team members and rarely got any playing time. Our job was to execute the upcoming opponent's offensive and defensive strategy while the starters played against us. This would help them get a feel for how our opponents would play in the upcoming game. Each week was filled with playing different offenses and defenses and to learn these plays, it often required us coming early so we could ensure we got them right.

I didn't fully understand it then, but this was key to our preparation for our next opponent. Each player on our team got to learn the tendencies of the player they would be guarding and they got an understanding of where they might end up in their most common offensive sets. Also, on offense, our team got to play against the scout team defense so they could also get a feel for what they would see on that end of the floor.

I would remain on the scout team for several years because I was usually at or near the end of the bench, but I learned to take pride in studying our opponents and doing my best to help our team prepare. This time was also advantageous because I got to play against our first team consistently, which only helped make me a better player. The statistics next to my name in the box score remained at zero, but I knew I was making a contribution to our team's success by helping them prepare in practice.

From the Bench

Another way to contribute is to help your teammates from the bench during games. Not only can you support them by simply standing for them when they come out of the game and be encouraging, but you can also talk to them when they come off the floor about what you see. I used my knowledge of the other team, from my experience as a scout team member that week in practice, to try and help them with some mistakes or tendencies I may have noticed. It could have to do with how they were guarding their opponent or things to do with their play in our team's offensive and defensive schemes.

When a player comes off the floor, they may not always be willing to listen to a coach, but they may make an exception to hear what you have to say. Even if they do hear what a coach says, sometimes when the same message comes from a peer, they may be more inclined to pay attention, especially if they respect you.

You should, however, beware that there will be moments where your teammates may not want to hear anything from you. I was the recipient of a few encounters where my teammates had some "choice" four letter words for me. You have to pick your moments and know when to approach your intended target and, more importantly, how to get your message across. All of this will help your teammates who do go in to the game and it will help you stay engaged in the action mentally so you will be ready when you are called upon.

Create an Identity

The most fun and effective way that I contributed to my team was when I helped create an identity for our bench during my junior season. I noted earlier about our team's struggles when I was a sophomore and how that year in practice we had lost almost every drill, competition and scrimmage to the starting group. I was determined not to let that happen again and to do this I felt we needed more connection between our bench players. That year I decided we needed an identity; we needed to take pride in our performances in practice and games and try to be a stronger unit. We needed a nickname to rally around and start to take more pride in our practice performance and recognize that our play had a huge impact on our team's success. So we took a nickname we had started using the year before, it is a nickname I took from the Sacramento Kings. The Kings had a solid bench in those years, filled with players who made huge contributions when they went in the game. We would from there on be known as they were; we were now the "Bench Mob."

Before we competed in scrimmages or drills, the second group huddled together and talked about what we were going to focus on to be successful, how we were going to play together as a group, communicate with each other and take it to our opponents (who happened to be the starters for our team). We created an "us against them" mentality that brought us together and caused all of us to play at our highest level because we were now playing for each other. We had suddenly given more meaning to our performances in practice because no one wanted to let anyone else down. We now had a team approach to our performances instead of an individual one.

While we didn't always manage to beat the first group, we got results because we were all working together toward the same goal. Previously it felt as if we were a group of individuals all trying to prove that we should be with the first group instead of being a "lowly second team player." I had been in practices before where guys would pout and be upset when they were taken off the first team and put with the second; it felt to them like a demotion. But we turned that thinking around with the creation of the "Bench Mob." It got to the point in my junior year where we loved being a "Bench Mob" member so much, that when coach told one of us to go play with the first group, we didn't want to do it. We were so tight as a unit that we wanted to compete together every day; now second unit guys got upset if they had to go play with the starters!

The "Bench Mob" translated nicely to games, too. After starting lineups were introduced, normally the starters who are announced form a huddle with the rest of the team around them. Before we did this with our starters, the "Bench Mob" would huddle together as a sign of solidarity and a reminder to each of us that we were going to be the difference in that night's game.

The effect that the formation of our "Bench Mob" had on our team was paramount. Not only did we become a stronger and better second unit, but the energy we created was infectious throughout the whole team. I learned the next season when I became a starter how much fun it was to play on a team where you feel like everyone wants the team to succeed, even if it means some players do not get the minutes they desire. It's an incredible feeling to make a positive play and hear your teammates on the bench rooting for you and getting excited because you are playing well, even guys on the end of the bench who never get a chance to play in game situations.

The positive results that the "Bench Mob" identity created had helped the first group prepare for the high intensity of games, raised the level of practice and helped us have a lot more fun in practice and on the bench. During my senior year, I used to hate when the second group, still calling themselves the "Bench Mob," beat us in practice. I knew it was good for us because you can't be a good team without a solid bench, but everyone in the gym hated losing; we were all now competitors and wanted to win. If you came into our practices, you would see players on our team battling each other. Everyone took pride in his own game and was not going to back down from anyone else. I witnessed several occasions where our starting forward and his back-up ended up on the ground, entangled in each other's arms, wrestling because neither was going to back down to the other. That competition is part of the reason that forward ended up becoming an All-American. His back-up contributed in practice by making him better every day, even when it meant getting under his skin and resulting in extremely physical play.

That competitiveness was a trait that ran throughout our whole team. We all challenged each other; nobody was going to back down to anybody else. If a guy on our team that day in practice wasn't playing their hardest or they were distracted for one reason or another, then someone else would call them out on it. They would challenge them to raise their level of play, because if they didn't, everyone would suffer. Our competitiveness led to everyone holding each other accountable for their effort in practice and it is the reason we ended up winning our conference. We were so sick of the challenges we gave each other that by the time we got to finally play in a game situation, we were happy to have a chance to beat up on someone else. We knew we would be successful because nobody could give us a challenge like we gave each other in practice. It made each of us better every day because we were consistent with it. We didn't just want to put the effort in to win on the days we felt good, we did it every day. This happened because of the type of players we had on our team that season. But I also believe the formation of the "Bench Mob" the previous year was what helped make our second group stronger, which led to more competitive practices and made us champions a year later.

Conclusion

There are so many ways to contribute to your team without producing big numbers on game night. Besides the examples I gave, you can also be a leader vocally in the locker room and in practice. From my sophomore to my senior year, I led our team out of every pre-game locker room talk with a prayer and a "pump up" speech. I would try to formulate words of motivation to get everyone even more excited to play in that game. There would be some nights after that speech I didn't play and others where I may have made a big contribution on the court, but no matter what happened with my playing time, I ensured in practice, the locker room and on the bench that I made a contribution to our team. I was going to help us win in any way possible. Whether I was a starter or the last player on the bench, I was going to have an impact on the game and our team's success.

Tips for Success

- You can make huge or great contributions to your team without playing a minute on game day.

- In practice, the locker room and on the bench you can help your team achieve success.

- Whether it is making observations during games, leading the second team in practice or being vocal in the locker room, there are many different ways to make an impact that do not show up in the box score.

Make it Happen

If you want to achieve your goals in the game of basketball, YOU have to make it happen. You cannot depend on anyone else to make your dreams come true; it is up to you, it is in your control. Wherever you end up will be the result of how badly you wanted to become your best. It will not always be easy, you cannot simply wish for something to happen and expect to have it come true without putting forth the necessary effort. There are ten different ideas in this book to help you reach your goals. It may take you doing all of them, it may take you doing less, but the bottom line is that you have to do something. Remaining at your current level of performance is not an option.

If you want to improve as a player and teammate, develop a plan of action, use what you have learned here to make sure you are making the most of every situation and taking advantage of all your opportunities and resources. If you do, you will find so much satisfaction with your results and you will become the player you always wanted to be. It will not happen overnight, but the journey you take to get there will be one that will help teach you many valuable lessons. You will continue to use these lessons as you move forward in your basketball career and any challenge you face, you will be able to draw upon what you have learned to guide you. You will be able to get past any obstacle that comes your way, nothing will be able to stop your pursuit of excellence.

The End Justifies the Means

We were beginning my senior season with an exhibition game at Maples Pavilion against one of the best college basketball programs in the nation. We were going head to head with Stanford University. As a young player, I had dreamt of stepping on this court. For me, this was the ultimate experience as a basketball player. The most exciting and special part of this game was that I had earned the starting point guard role. After four years I had finally made my way into the starting line-up because I followed every single one of the Bench Rules. I was now producing at the highest level I had ever reached as a player.

Everything was in slow motion as the announcer began to call the starting line-ups. It was the first time in my college career that I was part of it. It felt good to finally hear "Starting at guard, from Sacramento, California, number 24, Kevin Christensen." Everything I had done in the previous four years to improve led me to this point. All the moments I struggled, from barely being allowed to participate in practice as a freshman to being told by my coach I would never play for him, it all made this night that much sweeter. I felt validated as a player, I knew I had done so much and worked hard to earn my start that night. I had made it happen because of the many different avenues I took to improve every part of myself; I had gotten through many different challenges to get there. As it would turn out, though, I still had a few challenges ahead of me that I hadn't anticipated enduring. That start at Stanford was not the end of my time on the bench.

As ready as I was for this moment in my career, I would be forced to draw on the lessons I learned in the previous four years. The problem for me is that although I had done so much to become my best on the court, on this night at Stanford, I was awful. Because of my poor performance, I played the first four minutes of the first half and did not get back in the game until the end of the second half when we were already trailing by 25-plus points. I was back on the bench before my seat got cold. This would continue into the next two exhibition games against the University of Arizona and the University of San Francisco, both of which were also division one teams. It was so bad that I played three minutes at Arizona and did not even step on the court during the San Francisco game. It appeared that perhaps I was right back where I started, that I was again relegated to being one of the last players off the bench.

All I had been taught in my career made this situation one I was able to successfully handle. I could have easily let this defeat me, I could have thrown my arms in the air and given up mentally and physically. After all, I had years of struggle, defeat and utter despair on my side. It was not a situation where I was a freshman anymore. After that season my basketball-playing career looked to be over, I didn't have anymore time to wait for my hard work to pay off.

In the face of this adversity, I remained confident and knew I had been successful off the bench before, so there was no reason I couldn't, and wouldn't, do it again. I used the situation as continued motivation; I knew I was going to be a contributor in every possible way, just as I had learned to do my whole career.

In those next few weeks following our first exhibition games, I was still being the solid bench player I had learned to become. Because of my continued contributions in practices, games and the locker room, it would only be a short time before our head coach finally put me in my starting role for good. We had zero wins and three losses heading into our first two league games and our coach knew he had to make a change. He needed leadership and strong play at the point guard position and we both knew I was the man for the job. Once I entered the lineup, our team took off; we won ten of our next eleven games, with the only loss coming on a three point shot as time expired against Division I UC Santa Barbara. We suddenly became the team we knew we could be, and we continued our strong play to go on and win our conference for the first time ever. I was also recognized by the coaches in our conference who selected me to the all-conference team as we finished with a 16-4 record in CCAA (California Collegiate Athletic Association) play. My hard work to get off the bench was rewarded with a team and individual accomplishment, all of it because I was not satisfied with being mediocre, I wanted to be the best for my team and for myself, so I worked to make it happen. I had come a long way from just a few years prior when I was the last player off the bench.

Conclusion

You cannot let anyone else determine what your future will be in the game of basketball and how successful you will be as a player. You control your destiny; you will decide how far you go and how good you become. Learn from every situation you are put into and recognize that every challenge is a way to improve. Realize the importance that every player has on a team and place high value in yourself, your teammates and your coaches. Use the *BENCH RULES* as a guide, put them into action and begin to make your dreams happen on and off the court. The journey you take to be your best will challenge you, but you will ultimately make yourself and everyone else around you better for having experienced it. It is now time to stop wishing for positive results. It is time to go make it happen.

Tips for Success

- It is up to you to make your dreams become a reality on the court.

- Once you have taken full responsibility for yourself and future in basketball then you will start on your path to becoming great.

- Use and refer to BENCH RULES as a guide in your quest to becoming the ultimate player, teammate and person.

- It is time to stop wishing for better results, it is now time to go and make it happen.

Acknowledgements

It took many different people reading and contributing their ideas to make *BENCH RULES* a reality. Just as when I was a player I went to my coaches and teammates for their help and advice. Vince Inglima and Justin Clymo are the two people who I will forever be in debt to for their extensive work on making sure every little detail was handled in making this the best book it could possibly be. From editing to final cover and everything in between, this book was made infinitely better because of them.

A very special thank you to Steve Ball, Brandon Bronzan, Chris Ziemer, Mike Raudenbush, Sam Smith, Pat Fuscaldo, Rich Shayewitz, Jessica Smallman and Jay Flores for taking the time to read *BENCH RULES* and provide the type of constructive criticism that was necessary to make the message of the book clear, concise, and relative to any reader. Thank you to the Sports Information office at Sonoma State, particularly Brandon Bronzan and Tyler Lobe, for their contributions with statistics and providing information for every other random request I made.

This book is the result of 21 years of being involved in organized basketball. From my friends and family in Sacramento, my time at El Camino High School, Sonoma State University, Basket Clubs of Vienna with Coach George Libbon, and now at Sonoma Academy, so many different people have influenced me in so many positive ways. I have always been able to persevere through any adversity I faced to become a successful player, teammate, coach and person. For all of those who I have known throughout my time at my different stops and those who continue to influence me today I will forever be grateful to you. In particular I must single out my parents, brother and grandparents for their influences on me in every single step of my journey. It takes a solid foundation and many different people having a positive impact on a young person to help them become their best and all of you were instrumental in making this happen for me. No matter if I was successful or failed I knew you would always be there to support me. This support made me fearless in my pursuits of my dreams and there are no words or actions I could ever find that could thank you enough.

Appendix A
Timeline

In this book I have shown how the ten BENCH RULES can guide you to improving as a player in every aspect of basketball, on and off the court. The stories are not in chronological order, instead I jump around to relate certain stories from my playing career with each lesson. For that reason I have listed below a timeline of my playing career at Sonoma State University. I have included a brief description of each year and some of my statistics from that season, too. I rarely produced big numbers in the box score, but by using the BENCH RULES I made an impact that goes beyond traditional statistics.

Redshirt year (2001-02)- My first year at Sonoma State University. "Redshirt" is an NCAA term for student-athletes who attend school and practice with the team, but don't participate in games. This does not count toward the student-athlete's four years of NCAA eligibility. This enabled me to be a full-time student at SSU and a member of the basketball team. So, after this year was complete I still had all four years of eligibility. This redshirt year turned out to be a great thing for me as a player and a person. I was able to adjust to all aspects of college life and the struggle of living away from home for the first time.

Freshman year (2002-03)- This was a great year for us as a team. We qualified for the NCAA tournament for the first time in four years. I appeared in 13 of 28 games this season, and took 30 shots total on the year.

Sophomore year (2003-04)- A "rebuilding year" for Sonoma State Men's Basketball. This team featured just one senior and had many younger players who were depended upon for production. I played in 24 of 28 games and averaged 1.9 points in that time. In my 171 minutes (7.1 per game) that season I had a total of 16 assists and 12 turnovers.

Junior year (2004-05)- With the addition of some nice pieces from the junior college level and the growth of the SSU team members that returned, we had a solid team. We finished 16-11 and just missed out on the NCAA tournament. I played in 23 of 27 games and averaged 3.3 points per game. I was named co-MVP this season because of the actions I took to support my team in practice and on the bench during games. On a few occasions, I exploded for double-digit points in limited minutes off the bench.

Senior year (2005-06)- Our strongest year during my time at Sonoma State. I was inserted into the starting lineup three games into the season. We won our conference for the first time in twenty years and I was selected to the all-conference team. At the end of the season, I was voted the Most Inspirational Player for the fourth consecutive year and had the award named after me. I started 24 of 27 games, averaged 8 points per game and shot 39.3% from the three-point line. The biggest contribution I made on the court in my

23 minutes per game was in my assist to turnover ratio, which was 2.3 to 1 (115 assists, 50 turnovers).

Appendix B

BENCH RULES
Tips for Success

Believe in Yourself

- Always believe in yourself and your abilities. A player without confidence is one who is easily discouraged and becomes non-productive when things aren't going their way.

- The power of positive thinking will drive you to improving yourself. Negative thoughts and emotions will translate to your play on the court.

- Focus on what you are doing well. No matter how small an accomplishment may be, let it fuel you to continue improving.

- If you do not expect great things from yourself then you will settle for being mediocre.

Extra Work

- To become a better player you have to put in extra work in the off-season and during the season.

- Extra work means improving in the gym, the weight room, and in your mental capacity for the game.

- In-season you have to find time outside of your team's regularly scheduled practice to work on the necessary skills you need to become a better player.

- The off-season should be dedicated to becoming bigger, faster, stronger and smarter in all aspects of the game.

- Your coaches will have the best ideas for what areas can use the most improvement for you as an individual player. Your teammates rank a high second on this list.

- Your success on the court will be a direct result of the extra work you put into becoming a better player.

Never Quit

- If you are not happy in your situation you must realize the high costs quitting will have on your team and your future.

- Quitting can come in two different forms. It can be physically removing yourself from your team or giving up mentally.

- You only get so many chances in life to be a part of a competitive team. Do not waste these moments by being selfish and only thinking of yourself.

- There is great value in being a positive player and person no matter the circumstances.

- Quitting is the easy way out. Any one who has ever become their best as a player, teammate and person will tell you it was not easy to accomplish this feat.

Consistency

- Players are constantly judged by what they can consistently accomplish on the court.

- For your coach to put you in the game they need to know what you are going to make happen on a consistent basis. The greatest showcase for this is in practice.

- "Controlling the controllables" is about focusing on your effort and attitude, because they are the only two factors that you always have complete control over.

- A positive attitude and great effort are two traits that lead to success on and off the court.

Handle Outside Influences

- You must manage the effect that outsiders have on you regarding your view of yourself and your team.

- *Insiders* (coaches and teammates) see you in practice everyday and have a clear understanding of how you fit into your team's hierarchy and game plan.

- *Outsiders* (parents, friends, relatives, etc.) will often have a distorted view of reality. They will sometimes put others down to make you feel better. Their view focuses on your feelings and what they think is best for you, not what is always best for your team.

- Make sure your group of outsiders are positive and supportive individuals, and that you value the opinions of your teammates and coaches above all others.

Responsibility Off the Court

- The actions you take and the decisions you make outside the gym will have an impact on your performance in the gym.

- You may have to give up some of the things other people your age are doing, sacrificing that time so you can be fully prepared both mentally and physically for your next game or practice.

- Your spirituality, family and school are the only things that come before your sport and even those have to be managed properly to be a fully committed and responsible team member.

Utilize Every Opportunity

- Every second you are on the court, during practices, games, and workouts, is an opportunity to improve your game and status on your team.

- Practice is the biggest and best opportunity to prove that you should be playing in game situations.

- Practice must be approached with the same urgency as games. If you take this mindset you and your team will be stronger.

- You have to be ready at all times on game day. Stay mentally checked in to the game so you can perform successfully when you get on the court.

Love the Game

- Finding your love and passion for the game will make you a better player and an inspiration to everyone around you.

- Whether it is watching your favorite team play or a positive memory from your past, figuring out what brings you joy in the game will drive you to be your best.

- Love the game. Even the lowest moments for a player, when they are struggling and frustrated, can become a source of internal and external joy by simply loving the game and having a burning passion for it.

Embrace Your Role

- Every player has a role to play on a team. When these roles are recognized and accepted, then a team will be allowed to reach its full potential.

- It should be your goal to excel in your role, whether it is as a practice player or your team's top scorer.

- To figure out your role you may need some guidance; your coaching staff is the best source for this advice.

- To improve your status on your team you must thrive in your role. You cannot do this without first recognizing what that role is and embracing it.

Support Your Team in Different Ways

- You can make huge or great contributions to your team without playing a minute on game day.

- In practice, the locker room and on the bench you can help your team achieve success.

- Whether it is making observations during games, leading the second team in practice or being vocal in the locker room, there are many different ways to make an impact that do not show up in the box score.

Make it Happen

- It is up to you to make your dreams become a reality on the court.

- Once you have taken full responsibility for yourself and future in basketball then you will start on your path to becoming great.

- Use and refer to BENCH RULES as a guide in your quest to becoming the ultimate player, teammate and person.

- It is time to stop wishing for better results, it is now time to go and make it happen.

ABOUT THE AUTHOR

Kevin Christensen is a former basketball player and coach from Sonoma State University (SSU), an NCAA Division II institution in northern California. While at SSU, Kevin went from being the last player on the bench to an all-conference selection and California Collegiate Athletic Association champion. To this day the Sonoma State men's basketball program still gives the Kevin Christensen Award to the year's Most Inspirational Player. He followed up his collegiate career by playing professionally in Vienna, Austria. Kevin currently serves as assistant athletic director and head girls and boys varsity basketball coach at Sonoma Academy in Santa Rosa, California. Kevin and his wife Megan, along with their daughter Hannah, reside in Sonoma County.

Kevin can be e-mailed at BENCHRULES@gmail.com.